I0761544

Lost in Translation

LOST

in Translation

STEVEN HARVEY

The University of Georgia Press Athens and London

Published by the University of Georgia Press
Athens, Georgia 30602

Designed by Sandra Strother Hudson
Set in 10.5 on 14 Electra by G&S Typesetters, Inc.
Printed and bound by Maple-Vail
The paper in this book meets the guidelines
for permanence and durability of the Committee on
Production Guidelines for Book Longevity
of the Council on Library Resources.

Printed in the United States of America
01 00 99 98 97 C 5 4 3 2 1

Library of Congress Cataloging in Publication Data

Harvey, Steven, 1949 June 9–
Lost in translation / Steven Harvey.
p. cm.
ISBN 0–8203–1890–6 (alk. paper)
I. Title.
PS3558.A7195L67 1997
814′.54—dc20 96–31224

British Library Cataloging in Publication Data Available

Some of the essays in this manuscript first appeared in the following publications: *Creative Nonfiction*, *DoubleTake*, *Habersham Review*, *Iowa Review*, and *In Short*, a nonfiction anthology published by W. W. Norton.

For Barbara

Contents

Lost in Translation

Prologue

Every so often I get a letter from Margi, an artist and former student. The letters come in bright packages, each envelope, singular and intriguing as she is, signaling her moods. One, I see now looking through a stack of them, has my name and address in a strange boxy print with arrows and black bubbles all over it to guide and confuse the post office. Many are collages constructed out of images clipped from art books and magazines, bits of her world remade for mine.

My favorite has a large flower print with my name and address in

Gothic script taped to the side. When I open it I find that this was a page torn out of the calendar, the month of August printed on the inside, and within this is a card with the painting *The Wedding Meal* by Fourie, appropriate, Margi wrote, because it showed "an artist capturing catastrophe." The handwriting goes all around the painting and on into the card, her words chronicling her month of woes and joys and becoming a part of the design.

Margi is one of those rare and lucky people who sound like themselves in letters, perhaps because her talk is elaborate like writing, so she practices each time she speaks. "God is not the hero of a fairy tale to me," she writes, "but I'm not exactly sure who or what He is. Whatever or whoever, I think he's taken care of me well. Or it has—I have no point of reference." That's just the way she talks—backtracking often, correcting herself or rejecting a phrase, assertions tumbling into questions.

The gift in all this is that—in letters at least—I feel welcome to respond in kind. "God does not exist," I wrote back, "She happens." It is the kind of thing I would never say, but feel fine writing, at least in a letter to Margi, who liked the definition. She said it was a way of "defining something yet not caging it." That, in essence, is a way of characterizing our letters, too, which capture the part of ourselves that we can give away in words.

God has been happening to Margi a lot lately. Now in her twenties, she has anxieties about being an adult—"a feeling that you need to get your head together about a 'life plan' or something." She suspects that such worries sound humorous to someone more than twice her age, anticipating my smile as I turn her pages in front of the post office, but insists that the fears are real anyway, especially the daunting label of artist, which she hesitates to assume in the face of pitying looks from others. "I'm met with a sympathetic gaze," she writes, and "it scares me that maybe I *am* kidding myself."

The most important event since Margi left here—"it has truly changed my life," she wrote in one card—has been her trip to

Moscow as part of an artist exchange. Her letters, which usually bear the postmark of her university town, came for a while from a more distant horizon, filled with descriptions of Red Square and food lines and birch trees. In Russia, she reclaimed an essential part of her humanity that had gotten lost—become strange to her—in her home culture. In a foreign land she found a familiar face, and it was her own. "I felt," she wrote, "like I was seeing parts of myself I'd never seen before."

Margi's changes fascinate me. Miles and mountains away, I never see them, of course, but I get her translations of them, words for facts sent in the mail and folded in gift wrapping.

Robert Frost wrote that poetry, the life-blood of words, is what is lost in translation, but much of life comes to us just this way—as translation—with loss as the inevitable by-product. Lately I have had to wear glasses to read, getting all the world of words through the distortion of lenses. The sentences do not change, but *I* have, ever so slightly, since I wrote them or read them last, the lenses, measured in diopters, neatly recording how far short my sightedness has come. When I take the glasses off and look far out to the horizon, my view is clear, but I realize that all my life I have looked at the world through lenses of one sort or another.

I met my first girlfriend, in fact, over a telescope. Her father had set it up in his backyard—a five-inch lens, I recall—and had a line of neighborhood kids over to watch the stars. When my turn came, the scope was focused on Jupiter—the great planet a mere disk suspended in the depths of a black, unchanging night and surrounded by a speckling of moons. When I looked up from the glass, there she was, a preteen beauty delivered in the dark, her auburn hair, freckles, and moon-white skin borrowing and rearranging the components of the night sky for the adjusting lenses of my own eyes.

"Next," she said, smacking her gum and looking past me, but I hardly noticed. I went to the end of the line, awaiting another glimpse of these heavens.

"What you see is what you get," Annie Dillard wrote, but the unsettling corollary is that what you get sheds some of itself in the seeing. We never simply see the world as it is; rather, the world terminates in us and does so on our terms, while the world without us is lost in translation.

I don't think we like this at all, this feeling of being trapped in ourselves. Greedy for experience of the world beyond us, we grab wide, but take only what comes readily to hand. James Dickey has written that some of us commit suicide to shut off that endless voice—*our* voice—in our heads. We long for a new language—a foreign tongue—for discourse with ourselves. Like Victorians on holiday we leap at the opportunity to safari far from home only to find that the game at the end of the sights of our elephant gun is someone in a funny hat and jodhpurs who looks a lot like us.

Sometimes—thank God—we are shaken from the complacency of turning the world into ourselves. By luck the translation keeps the poetry of the original and the familiar takes on a genuine strangeness. "It's in the people who pass you on the streets," writes Margi from Moscow, "the buildings you've seen in photos your whole life long, and even in the moon that overlooks an unfamiliar city half a world away." Such moments though are rare, the defining events of our lives. "You look," Margi adds, "and find your reflection—only much clearer than before." At such times, we are twice blessed, getting more of the world *and* more of ourselves than we deserve.

Most books of personal essays celebrate the self—the individual isolated from the rest of society, isolation being the dominant theme of the personal essay since Emerson's paean to individualism in "Self-Reliance" and Thoreau's famous retreat to the cabin at Walden Pond. We are, as Americans, drawn to these idiosyncratic and at times downright quirky visions of the individual because it is part of the myth of self that we live by.

It is not, however, the way we form a self. None of us is born and nurtured in isolation. Instead, we discover who we are — as Socrates taught us — by engaging in dialogue with others, constantly translating the self we were in the context of new situations and new people. We create a self by means of these translations, engaging differences, questioning assumptions, changing slightly who we are, and shedding in equal proportion who we can no longer stand to be. We speak, we listen, we adjust our voices — whether we read the voices on the page or hear them in the street.

Sometimes these translations of self are public business, like an argument at a ball game or a book sent into the world. At other times, they are as private as the poet fashioning fresh words out of the hush created by all the voices in her head. These translations of self often occur when cultures meet, but the exchange can be close to home as well, over the dinner table, for instance, or in the bedroom of a husband and wife. Something is lost, of course, in the translation — an old self whom we recognize with a shake of the head or a sneer or, if we are generous, a laugh, and yet, such losses are precisely the kind by which, according to the ancient paradox, we are found.

The chapters in this book take on a variety of topics that range somewhere between the proximity of backyard football games and the otherness of ancient Tibetan music, each piece written to stand alone as a separate essay. One essay examines homelessness from the all-too-comfortable confines of a warm home. Another speculates on lives unlived as a way of learning how to live the one that, after all, happened. Students become the teachers in one chapter and then leave the teacher behind, which is only right. There is, as well, an essay on the essay that illustrates that the form is the finest vehicle for the expression of individualism precisely because it is the perfect place to sort out the contending voices that make up a single voice we can live with.

Separate as the essays are, they all tell the same story, and though they bear different titles they all could be called "Lost in Translation." Margi, herself, returns anonymously in one of them, still asking about God. In each essay, the self is brought against a new world or two worlds are brought into conflict, the soul shedding a husk of its former life in the encounter. Such losses, the essays say, are the leavings of our changes and the price we pay for becoming.

Some part of our true selves, I'm convinced, finds voice only in such translations—in engagement with others on others' terms—and I suspect that it is the part of us that we cannot live without. "Our letters," Margi wrote at one point, "say a lot about our souls," aware that if God shows up at all in our lives, She is between the lines. Naming has always been our job. If we can translate our silences, finding on the tips of our tongues the changed name of God in our time, then we can live with the simple fact that all else will inevitably be lost. We can live through this autumn, and another autumn, and the last autumn, too.

Another Autumn

Every October something in the air brings back one brilliant autumn afternoon from my first year living in North Georgia. There was plenty of beer that day, and before the day was done, my wife, Barbara, and I found ourselves shoved in a jeep with six or seven other happy revelers headed straight up a mountainside. We were young but didn't know it, the two of us having suddenly assumed the twin responsibilities of work and a child, believing, after pacing the floor many nights in a row with a crying baby in our arms and long days ahead, that we had left our own youth far behind.

But this was Oktoberfest in the Georgia mountains and we were headed for the sky. Leaves formed a canopy of colors — reds and browns and yellows — that hid our destination, a bright, blue vista. It hid all that we had left behind as well though we knew that the valley and other mountains were laid out just beyond our view. It hid us for a moment from our changes, too. Free of the baby, we were on a date again, and Barbara buried her face in my jacket and shrieked like a kid herself as the jeep roared up the logging trail.

Who knows what brings this memory to mind? The mulch-rich scent of October, perhaps, delivering whole a time when an old sense of self had yielded incompletely to a new one, in a new place. We shouted and laughed and held our hats as we bounced over gullies and clattered over rocks, dust billowing behind us, the banner of our irrepressible joy.

So it goes — the senses shake loose memories that shade, like veils, the present, rendering today strange and transforming any familiar spot into a mystery. The yard beside the house of my wife's family near Charlotte, North Carolina, is such a place, the site of the Hupfer-Harvey Holiday Games, backyard father-son football contests conducted at Thanksgiving and Easter. The rosters are short and nepotistic — my brother-in-law and our sons. "Harvey throws, Harvey receives, and Harvey makes the tag" — my younger boy, Sam, shouted after one play.

To compensate for our small numbers we cheat, tossing forward laterals with abandon to create a volatile playing space. Triple reverses, sneak plays, intentional fumbles, quick snaps, and the pigskin-hidden-under-the-sweatshirt dash are also common. Once in every game, the fathers move the ball back a few yards while the sons are in a huddle, a trick that fooled the boys and later tickled the teenagers. Now it brings nothing but groans to the lips of our collegians, but we still do it.

For the first few years we controlled the contest, letting the kids pick up a few touchdowns before we threw our weight around and trounced them. Barbara's father, our sole fan when he was alive, watched the antics from the sunlit sidelines, smiling under the shadow of his fedora. By the time the boys entered high school we began to lose, and now that they are high-school graduates we simply look bad, bent over and gasping for breath after our golden-legged sons have set us off balance with a simple feint and a dash for the line. We—the weary dads—console ourselves after a game with a few beers, talking of halcyon days when we left the tykes in the dust and inventing revenge scenarios, hopeful now because the boys are college men, initiates in the life of debauchery, and because we have recruited young Sam, the first and only draft pick in this very little league.

Sam—the future—is ours, and his presence reminds us of when the other boys moved with his artless grace in the early stages of mastering the game. Sometimes when I hand-off the ball and watch him race for the goal it is the older boy I am watching and a former me I am remembering. I fool myself into thinking I'm less sore and winded than I am and half suspect, when I look to the sidelines, that I'll see Barbara's dad again smiling under the shadow of his hatbrim.

The leaves of one season mix with another in the mind, and the thoughts of one autumn day bring back memories of another golden afternoon more than a decade ago when we made apple juice with Alice and Jo—friends of ours for many years. All morning the leaves had been tumbling out of trees and piling up against the house, while the kids and I, in sweaters and jeans, gathered up the last of the windfall apples from a tree in our yard, a tree famous for juicers, Jo assured me. We loaded the lumpy grocery sacks into the station wagon and headed down the road, fruit spilling and rumbling into the floorboards with each bump and turn.

Alice and Jo's place at Crow Gap is the most beautiful patch of land in our valley of creeks, meadows, mountain laurel, and hardwood stands. If there is a corner of Eden left in our grease-stained world, it is here. The house is modest—a small, high-pitched, wood frame building with a porch at the back. The yard, dotted with shrubs and plantings, is darkened here and there by enormous oaks, maples, and poplars with gnarled, exposed roots that ruckle the lawn. Beyond all that is a pasture nibbled on by the horses, Roberta and Miss Boo, and tended otherwise by Jo, the kind of open field where kids can run and run in knee-high grasses, never it seems coming to the end but falling somewhere midway in a laughing pile. And beyond *that,* heaped against it all like the curved arm of a sleepy beast, is a ridge of mountains that alternately holds the sun and the moon in its crook.

We set up the apple press in the side yard that day while kids ran down to the creek, flapping their arms and cawing aloud to scatter the crows. By that time Alice's dog Found was lost, but Lost was still around, sniffing at our pantlegs. Adults took turns on the crank, pommelling the apple quarters that Jo dumped into the box. Puffing and wheezing we told jokes about bad apples and apple polishing and someone being rotten to the core, and speculated about ways to speed up the fermentation time of cider, Jo grinning and cackling with each crack, and all the while the juices flowed out of the barrel of the press, down a wooden shunt, and into buckets to be hauled to the porch.

Alice and Barbara kept busy coring apples on the porch, Alice telling stories and smiling, always smiling, and as the buckets were delivered to their feet, they began straining the juice for scum, leaving the pommies for flavor, and poured the finished product into milk jugs on the picnic table. We worked until dusk, shadows spreading on the lawn and thinning to a general darkness, and watched as the mountain horizon slowly released a harvest moon that rolled like a pumpkin into the sky. When we were done, kids came in from play and adults folded down their shirt sleeves as they sauntered back to the porch, ready to crown our achievement by downing glass after glass of the sweetest apple juice that any of us—we all agreed—had ever tasted.

Barbara and I had been in the mountains for five years by this time, living in the place long enough to know its weather. We had begun to understand the rituals of the year, learning by simply staying put the palpable sense of time passing. Years had gone by since that first Oktoberfest, and we couldn't have imagined ourselves without the noisy children, and though we sometimes hatched plans to move back to North Carolina where Barbara had grown up, we knew, with each late-night return to the valley after a trip, that this place in North Georgia was home.

Three or four years after that apple afternoon, at the end of another autumn, Alice died of cancer, living her final months in an apartment in town. Barbara had given birth to Sam, our third child, by then so we bundled him up and brought him for a visit. Alice would have loved Sam, the most rambunctious and affectionate of our children, the kind of eleven-year-old who announces himself as home by letting the door slam behind him, dropping his books on the floor, and shouting "Pizza!" It breaks my heart that she did not know him. She had been very sick when we arrived—had not spoken all day—but when Barbara, fighting to keep a smile on her face, held the baby above the bed, Alice raised her head from the pillow, a monumental effort, gave him a kiss on the cheek and closed her eyes.

After we said our goodbyes, we bundled up the baby and walked out into a night that, in memory, was dank and cold, though that may be a mistake, the emotions of that evening changing the weather in my mind. Who knows? I pulled my coat collar up and followed Barbara to the car, kicking senselessly at the leaves piled along the edge of the road. Several days later our friend died, and there is an empty place in our town still. Two years later when Barbara and I had our last child we named her Alice.

Not long ago the Walter H. Rich building, where I taught for fifteen years, was torn down—thus becoming another memory. It was, I'm sure, the humblest academic building in America—a one-story, red-brick affair with two wings, an incongruously columned cement porch, and a hand-painted sign above the door. Inside, the building had one hall, several offices, four classrooms, and bad plumbing. Despite its lowly look it was the shrine to literature on our campus, housing the English department, which kept a plunger handy and went about its celestial business with little regard for worldly affairs, or anything else for that matter, unless the pipes backed up.

The building once housed the Home Economics classes, and there were holes in the floor that had at one time accommodated pipes for stoves and sinks and such. "Don't Feed the Animals" a clown had written in magic marker around one hole. "They Bite." There were other signs of shabbiness as well. One of my colleagues dutifully hung posters each year, arranging them so that they appeared to be there for decoration when in fact they covered holes, this time in the walls. Each year a few new ones would appear, as plaster fell away, calling for more posters so that by the end of our stay the rooms were beginning to look like billboards for the bards.

Old and venerable, Rich had its share of mysteries and oddities. The closet-sized bathrooms, which had no hot water and no soap unless the department head brought a couple of bars from home, were not hard to find because late one night some joker stepped barefoot in pink paint, wandered through the building, and ended up in the women's bathroom. For years two pink footprints were planted in front of the woman's commode, facing out. Not to be outdone, the men got together and blazed a blue trail to the other bathroom, the footprints at the commode facing the other way, of course.

Our buildings grow on us—we wear them every day—and no matter how dilapidated they are, a sentimental attachment to the brick and wood where we spend our lives is inevitable. The new building—all metal, glass, and thunderous noise—went up just outside the scarred windowsills of our classrooms, adding inaudibility to injury. It did not seem very friendly. Rich, on the other hand, had the familiar shabbiness of an old friend. During its last year wrens built a nest in the pyracantha bush outside my office window, and, with the building lapsing into disrepair, I began to think of it as a nest, too, cozy, fragile, and temporary. With the end at hand, the college stopped making all but necessary repairs, so when ceiling tile came loose after a rain it was not replaced, and with holes above as well as below and beside us, the place increasingly looked and felt like a bunker. I found myself eyeing warily the remaining tiles when I walked to class, humming the theme music from *The Alamo*.

Just before the wrecking ball came crashing into Rich, there was a frenzy to save things. The old sign hangs in our library, and all of us took bricks home, attempting to hold on to some memories of the place and ourselves. The bricks do nothing for me, but the other night walking past the spot where my office had been, I suddenly stopped. Trees and buildings had changed and the pyracantha with the nest was gone, but something about the curve of the road brought the old scene back, and I was in my second or third year of teaching again, walking home after exams while Marlin Wilbanks, who had waited three hours for his grade to be posted on my office door, whooped for all eternity to hear at his "A," though the building, the sidewalk, and the door upon which the grade was posted are all gone.

Lately I have been interested in a phenomenon, nameless and without a shrine, that is like memory but goes beyond it. I'm thinking about moments that have the feel of a memory though they have no apparent source in our lives. Memories that have forgotten who they are, reveries with no specific object.

I have had these moments of introspection all my life. On a bright September day years ago in Charlotte I stopped and was suddenly mesmerized by a common sight: a birdbath filled with standing water. A few crisp leaves clung to the edge of the scum while their soggy companions overlapped in layers underwater, the deepest of them sunk in mud with only a curl of color here and there waving dimly in the sepia dark. The city buzzing all around me, I stood entranced, gazing long into muck the color of the inside of a closed eye. Not grounded in any event, the oddly arresting occasion released me, like magic, from the present without returning me to the past.

More recently I was brought up short by a gutter under a row of maples near the office where I teach, the curb tilted in such a way that the winter snow melt could not drain and the leaves of several seasons floated there suspended and still. Like those who see a familiar face they cannot place, I looked deep past the wind-rippled surface of my reflection to all that stillness below—a stillness like the depths of space or the abyss in the iris of a lover. Who knows how long I stood there? A minute, I guess. I shook myself and walked hurriedly on, a little ashamed at a private moment so publicly exposed, taking with me the darkened image of my face on water and leaving behind a circle of brown.

These moments of detached contemplation, of evanescent feeling—these sensations are not true memories but are delivered by the same mechanism as memory, registering in the mind and evoking emotions in the same way that something in the air in October brings back a brilliant fall day. Detached from any specific past, they take me to a part of the mind that is timeless and eternal, the fountainhead of the spirit.

Any wind, chime, or shoreline will do, any path winding into the woods. They are an affect without an object. Or, put another way, they are all subject. Dense subjectivity. Suspended in a silence akin to the one that surrounds me now as I write, they are the source of my own creativity. Unlike memories anchored in family or friends or football, which give us a sense of belonging among others, these dumb mnemonics of the spirit remind me that we are abandoned in the world, uncomfortably wedged between the two eternities of our grander home.

It is possible that these memories without a past have a hidden motive — a subtle source or combination of sources — that the conscious mind has simply forgotten. It may be that the autumnal revery inspired by leaves floating in water goes back to dark afternoons at the North Carolina house when I would help Barbara's dad clean the gutters, but I don't think so. The sight that stops me — transports me, as if cut loose for a moment from time and this world — does not, after all, take me back to that house, but to a set of broodings that seem to have been a part of my mental equipment from the beginning. I am drawn to the sight of these clogged gutters of the spirit by something already in me, something true and intrinsic to me, the part of me that inevitably emerges if I am alone long enough.

All this sentiment is easily dismissed, I realize, as sentimentality — dismissed as the pastoral version of crying into your beer — or worse, understood as an archetypal experience and explained away with codified primordial symbols. "A pool," says my friend who is taking a dream-therapy course. She cocks her eyebrow. "A *dark* pool," she adds meaningfully, sizing me up as another dreamer gone awry. "Hmm." The difference between her and me, though, is that I don't want to understand the experiences. I want to *have* them. I want to be there — alive to these serendipitous moments — and in that sense *know* them. It is the way I feel about literature, another kind of daydreaming. If such dreams have a source in something sexual, sociological, or archetypal, fine, but that is not why I care about them.

If memories place us among the faces we know from another time, these memory-less memories are valuable because they tell us who we aren't and locate us in forever. Unstoried reminders that there is a self beyond history, beyond the self I live with, they stop me — as the saying goes — dead, tugging at the part of me that I do not earn, the only part of myself that I cannot lose or give away, the source of the identity that claims me when the disguises of society are shed. Such reveries, no doubt, are a comfort to the old, offering a glimpse of the self they meet on the deathbed when the faces of loved ones turn away—the self that *they* can barely live with, the self beatified.

If I look past the floating leaves and into the darker ones embedded in the mulch, this ancient version of me emerges, the hollow-eyed image that will not go away. Such looking takes little more than a glance, but it is potent. Heaven, it says, will not be like earth. It will, instead, stop you for no reason the way this darkness has. You will let go of football and apple dreams and the happy rituals of October. You will let go of work and home and friend and child and lover. You will stop before the dark eye of the universe, the robes of memory falling away, and, in less than a breath, an eternity will pass.

Moonbright
through the torn shade—
the milky way.

ISSA

Lost in Translation

"Like me," Junko says, pulling the flaps of her kimono around her, and I imitate the gesture with my robe, crossing my arms—first left and then right—over my heart. Next she turns to Matt who, all elbows, hesitates before he gets it right—our instincts tell us to wrap these things the other way. At last, he tightens the obi with a flourish and stands back, looking like a cross between a featherweight boxer and a ballerina. Sam in Ninja pajamas leaps from a sofa, kicking and slicing the air in imitation of television warriors, needing no instruction apparently in the ways of the East, and Alice, dressed earlier, pads in looking like a tiny geisha.

Once we are taken care of, Junko turns her attention to Nessa and Barbara who are still lost in bright prints. She tells them to go the other way with theirs—right and then left. "Like me," Junko says again, opening and closing her kimono the opposite way for them. "Yes," she says, smiling, when at last we all get it right. Clothed in strangeness, we look at each other and laugh.

Wearing traditional Japanese robes in the den of our house in Georgia, my family does look strange. All of us, I notice, move our arms in slow, wide gestures like dancers, getting used to the feel of the open sleeves floating beneath our hands, and there is the subliminal urge—with arms extended this way—for us, so suddenly strangers, to hug each other. Kimonos can be traced to ancient Chinese dress and are largely unchanged since the discovery of silk more than 2,000 years ago. In them we float, transported out of time and place by the liquid turning of brightly colored prints. We are, indeed, clothed in strangeness, and by this we can begin to measure how strange we must seem to the one who brought the gifts.

Junko, an exchange student, has come from Tokyo to our tiny mountain town in Georgia to live with us for a year. Her name, so odd on our lips, means "charming child," and it is easy to see that she is charming—she moves among us, our strange blond selves, with such familiarity. "Very good, very nice," she chirps, patting us on the lapels. It is also easy to tell from her nervous English that she is—despite her sixteen years—just a child and 3,000 miles from home and her own language.

After all, she looks normal in a kimono—it clings happily to her and rides with, not against, her arms and torso when she moves. She simply wears it. On us the robes feel ceremonial and our bodies—scarecrows in silk—resist the seductions of their folds. We look goofy, an American family lined up stiffly this way, and I doubt that we make Junko feel more at home. Still, she plays along, and lifting a slender wrist to her mouth, joins in with our laughter, while the sleeve of her kimono falls casually across her elbow.

"A girl born half a world away is sleeping in the bedroom overhead," I told Barbara after we settled in bed that first night — just a sentimental thought. But it wasn't long before the difference — the realization that Junko was from another world — became palpable. Every morning at 6:30 her wooden shoes clonked down the steps, and at night, when she bathed, the house filled with a sweet, lotus scent. We held our own, of course. Sam still terrorized us as usual with the plastic weaponry of the American West, and I banged out country tunes on the guitar. It was still our house. But we felt, nonetheless, a difference in our midst.

An early assignment in school found Nessa, my fifteen-year-old daughter, sitting beside Junko at the kitchen table, sorting and identifying leaves — the girls' differences readily apparent. Nessa's blonde hair tumbles midway down her back; Junko's hair, even longer, drops in straight, black strands. The skin of Nessa's freckled arm is bluish and slightly translucent, while Junko's skin is smoother, a buttery surface that holds light. Cutting labels, Nessa flings her scissors about in the air, her body relaxing into a loose, open posture, legs spread, elbows out. When she talks to us she looks over her shoulder and throws her head back gayly. Junko methodically pastes the leaves on paper, her gestures smaller — a quizzical nod, a lifting of eyebrows, a twisting of the upper body while knees stay firmly together.

Both girls chatter happily, but Nessa's laugh is explosive and her English — a lifelong friend — dances unfettered on her lips. Junko's laugh is a sweet sing-song, and her English wears robes.

"This one?" Junko asks.

"Uh, oak," Nessa says. "Yeah, that's an oak."

"Oak, good." Junko lifts the next leaf. "This one?"

"That's . . . ah," Nessa flips through the tree book. "This one right here—sassafras."

"Sassarass, good. This one?"

Two weeks after Junko arrived, Barbara and I loaded a guitar and some big boxes into the minivan and took Matt—our oldest child—to college for his first year. The ten-hour drive to Charlottesville seemed endless, and I don't remember anything about it except the cassettes—Beatles, Cat Stevens, U2—the least common denominator of our musical tastes. Soon enough we had exhausted the sounds we could share and contented ourselves with silence. Sad as we were, we knew it was time for Matt to leave—in part our silences told us so.

I had gone to graduate school at Virginia only five years before, and Charlottesville had changed little. After the parent orientation was done, Barbara and I had time alone so we walked our old streets, fighting off the urge to say "I remember when" but feeling it at each familiar turn of the sidewalk. We walked past the Colonnades and the park where I played football with Matt and the other kids. We walked past the lights of fraternity row where the family and I on Saturday mornings would clamor beneath sleeping undergraduates on our way to read the latest graffiti painted on Beta Bridge. We walked past Beta Bridge, hidden under a thousand Friday night messages, and I wondered how many layers of paint I would have to chip away to get back to the graffiti of our lives. The next day we took Matt to breakfast and strolled across the old campus one last time. Then we brought him back to his dorm and watched him walk away. In a moment he was gone and we drove off, the silence in the car like a fresh coat of whitewash over all our words.

Barbara and I tried to take the sting out of the good-bye by staying in an old, grand hotel in Abington, Virginia, for a few days, basking in the luxury of drinks and peanuts on the porch and Braves games on the TV. We found a trail along the embankment of an abandoned train line, the Virginia Creeper, and spent an afternoon walking down it and back, freed from memories by the newness of our surroundings. We talked about the future most of the time—a conscious effort, I think.

That night, on some excuse, we called Matt, but his phone just rang. A good sign, we said, though the rings resonated in some hollow place in me. When we called the girls at home we got giddy voices and learned that Nessa needed something sewn to her band uniform and that Junko had allergies.

It was time to get home.

At home we found that Junko was learning the cost of change. Her eyes were swollen and nose red from pine pollen in our area. In the mornings she woke looking puffy like a prizefighter and at night she plowed through a box of tissues, sniffing constantly and saying "I hate, I hate." Despite her willingness to change, a part of her resisted the pollinated air of her adopted country. Later when she caught poison ivy for the first time and walked through the house saying "itchy! itchy!," I feared she would give up and ask to go home.

Colloquial English took a toll, too, and, like a pruritic, served as a stubborn reminder that this was not Japan. So when she heard a fellow student say "I busted my ass," she thought it was a fine American expression. Unfortunately it did not go over so well when she delivered it to a teacher on a field trip. For Junko, the air in America was thick with invisible demons, all that glittered turned dangerous, and the ground was hard.

During the first days of school, there was something in the air for Barbara and me, too, and we found ourselves moping about the house at times. For a while we avoided Matt's room, knowing, I guess, how we would react to the hopelessly obvious metonymy of empty shelves. Bright kimonos and ukatas, the smell of lotus, and the friendly chirpings of a charming child didn't help.

In Charlottesville, I had picked up a book on Japanese kana, the ideogrammatic writing of Japan, and began studying the language. It was hard at first to make my lines follow the shapes of those in the book. This was not just lettering, it seemed, but drawing too, some kana requiring many strokes, the strokes of each kana made in a certain order and a certain way. It did not help to watch Junko who drew the kana with such ease, the many strokes of the word *kimono*, for instance, done surely and effortlessly. When I sat down with my Japanese book I felt like Alice, my first grader, who was struggling to print "come" and "go."

I learned that Japanese is a language filled with strangeness, since much of the written form goes back, like the kimono, to ancient China. When Junko counts to ten in her language she speaks Japanese, but writes those words in ideograms older than the words she speaks and borrowed from a foreign tongue. This layering of the familiar on the alien, common to all modern languages, began for Japan in the seventh century and is such a powerful feature of Japanese that a second kind of alphabetical writing eventually was developed as a way to bridge more naturally the gap between writing and speech. To Junko all this seems as common as Greek prefixes do to us, but to the outsider there is a special excitement to these ancient shapes. American poets like Ezra Pound were fascinated with the way that anyone—even those who don't know the language—can look into these images and, peeling back the accrued definitions of subsequent cultures, gain some intuitive sense of their original meaning. With them the poet in us can look through the strange to the graffiti of all souls.

Finding the familiar in the strange is as human as sex and as old as poetry, the delight of differences followed by the shuddering recognition of a shared humanity. We find this paradox in the sonnet, a poem with a turn or surprise just past the halfway mark that is often resolved in the final couplet. But the most compressed form of this kind of wisdom is haiku. A sonnet fills silence; haiku keeps it. A sonnet binds differences together; haiku lets go of them at the same time.

This ancient Japanese form of letting go has its source in love letters—more precisely, the letters of a departed lover. No one is sure how the custom began, but by the tenth century, poetry was the mode of discourse in court society and lovers were expected to exchange haiku-like poems after an evening tryst. It is hard for us to imagine this now, men gathering up their clothes and shoes before dawn in order to slip away from lovers without being seen. They would dash across the courtyard in brightly colored hunting robes while tucking hair in the lacquered topknot worn by nobility at the time and—safely returned to quarters, their feet still wet from the dew—would pen a love poem on fine paper, which was knotted and marked and sent, sometimes with a flower, before the morning was out. No poem meant no next night—that was the convention. "Indeed," wrote Sei Shonagon, the most observant of these courtesans, "one's attachment to a man depends largely on the elegance of his leave-taking."

Great stuff!, I thought, after several nights spent reading *The Pillow Book* of Shonagon and the other stunning source of these poems, *The Tale of Genji* by Murasaki Shikibu. *Genji* is particularly good. The world's first novel, it tells of the exploits of a "frighteningly" handsome but sensitive prince with many lovers. Moonlight, evening dew, cherry blossoms, and love—these are the subjects, all that shimmers and disappears.

The poems in these books were not true haiku—not yet. That would come later when these same court lovers divided the longer poetic form, the tanka, into question and answer games, and the answers were in the strict syllabic form that we call haiku. But haiku borrows much of its imagery from these early poems, and the haiku's theme of the evanescence of things clearly has its source in these notes written by lovers who had spent the night wrapped in each other's kimonos and curled in each other's arms.

Great stuff, indeed!

The morning after I closed the covers on Genji I left a poem about mist and highways and ankles in sheets for Barbara, folded it with some bedraggled flowers and put it on her pillow.

Needless to say, she was amused.

Armed with my book of Japanese kana and her calculator-like word-finder, Junko and I sat at the dining room table and translated haiku—at least, we tried. I printed a transliterated version of the haiku on the page in front of us and Junko read through it, her hand opening and closing as she counted off the syllables with her fingers.

"Yes, haiku," she said, when her fingers closed into a fist at the end of the five-syllable last line. She scratched the poison ivy under her eye and began writing English words above the Japanese. Over the word *ana* she wrote "hole" and over *ya* she wrote a colon.

"Haiku very boring," she said, opening her eyes wide as she always does when she is excited. "But if you see in your mind—is okay."

Above the syllable *no* she wrote "'s" but stumbled on the word in front of it. "Shoji," she whispered, "how say *that*." Eyes wide, she typed quickly into her word-finder. "Shoji like sliding door," she mumbled, "but. . . ." Then she showed me the definition on her machine: "A sliding door with a piece of Japanese paper on a lattice."

"Not good for Sam," she added with a giggle. She brought her hand down in a mock karate chop and said, "Bam."

"That's for sure," I said.

She wrote "sliding door" and the word "then" above the long first word in the first line and "milky way" above the last word in the poem.

"Ama-no-gawa," I said in her language, haltingly, like a child—the word, not a word for me, but a plaything on my tongue.

"Mil-ky way," she answered. "Yes."

After a half hour of poking around at this text, our literal translation of Issa's immortal haiku looked like this:

Then:
Sliding door's hole's
Milky way.

We both examined the sheet for a while, not sure what to do next—this was our first experiment in translating haiku, and the results seemed, well, meager.

"Words and meaning are very different," she said, apologetically. "You must picture."

Despairing of any verbal solution, she drew a stick figure picture of a person under a window with a hole in the shade. Then she drew several lines from the hole to the man.

"Moonlight," she said, still drawing the lines—as if the figure were bathed in it. "Moonlight."

I looked back at her puzzled and pointed out that there was no mention of moon in the poem.

"Always moon in haiku—if night, always moon. I *sure*." She scratched the poison ivy again just under the rim of her glasses. "Every peoples in Japan know this shoji and this moon," she said. "I *sure*. Must picture moon."

She looked at me and opened her eyes wide again, as if I might look through them and see what she sees. For a moment we shared what is lost in translation.

Cricket—
did you lose your voice
or become it?

BASHŌ

What is lost in translation? What is the rate of exchange? What do we take with us and what do we leave behind? Bashō, the great seventeenth-century Japanese poet, knew. He lived in a shack and spent the last years of his life wandering about the Japanese countryside, visiting sites whose names were familiar to him from poetry—translating the words back into places. "He go walking all the time," was the way Junko put it. Bashō said: "The months and days are the travelers of eternity." Before leaving on one journey, he tacked a sign on his door saying that "even a thatched hut" can become "a doll's house."

Yes, he knew.

A field, a temple, a view—anything he passed might bring to mind the poem of some former master and Bashō would respond with a poem of his own. The past challenged him and kept him fresh and clever. The famous names of the Eight Views of Lake Omi, for instance, had been said in a well-known thirty-one syllable tanka. After seeing the views, Bashō was challenged by friends to condense all eight of them into a seventeen syllable haiku, a poem less than half the size of the original tanka. One of the "views" was the gong of the bell at Mii temple, so Bashō wrote this:

Seven views were lost
in mist when I heard
the temple bell.

Even the original of this poem, then, is a translation, one that wins us because of its losses. In the poem we "see" the views of Lake Omi in the same way that we "see" the sound of the temple bell, a reminder of the simple truth that seeing is insight and originates from ourselves, a lesson worth savoring. And yet, the losses cannot be denied—the names of all those views are gone. In the mists of any translation, something inevitably gets left behind.

Of course, Bashō challenged others to translate him, as well. His most famous poem is an early one he wrote when he and friends, after a long silence, heard a frog flop into the water. According to tradition, the poem was composed spontaneously. "Kawazu tobikomu mizu-no-oto," Bashō suddenly blurted out when the frog leapt, the phrase fitting perfectly the last two lines of a haiku. After entertaining several possible opening lines from his friends, Bashō settled on this, here in one of the translations that Junko and I devised:

Small pond:
tiny frog jump
happy water-sound.

This little poem is still known by every school child in Japan, and Junko knows it by heart in Japanese, but it is not the only famous frog haiku. Issa, writing a century later, answered the old master's poem this way:

Skinny frog,
don't budge—
Issa is here!

"Issa is here!" the poem claims, as Bashō had himself announced to the poets before him. I am with you to help and carry on with the struggle, yes, but I am also here to take your place. *That* is the art of translation, and that, of course, is what is lost as well.

When asked by his friends at the end of his life to write a death poem, Bashō answered that all of his poems were death poems. Later, according to tradition, he did write one. The translation that we came up with goes like this:

Sick of walking
I left the landscape
to my dreams.

In translation, we get to keep the dreams, perhaps—it is for dreams that Bashō himself left the hut—but no matter what we do, the sick traveler, the human being we love, stays behind.

pond:
frog—
plop!
BASHŌ

One night Nessa took Junko to a clearing in the woods behind our house to look at the stars. The lights of Tokyo, and most of Japan, are so bright that she had never seen the Milky Way—the "ama-no-gawa"—before. It had been raining for several days and the skies had just cleared, so the girls slipped into jackets and hiked to the knoll.

I thought of Junko's name. In Japanese it means charming child, but the more ancient etymology of the Chinese ideogram for her name means "wet woods." It seems odd for a city girl from the Orient to be led into the woods by a blonde girl from Georgia, odd, yes, but as her name suggests, it is a kind of homecoming as well. We are all at root, the same, her name tells me, as Junko in miniskirt and high wooden shoes ducked under the dripping limbs and hobbled on the mulch path behind the khaki coat and blue jeans of my country daughter.

"Is very beautiful," Junko said when she came back later, her hair wet, her eyes big with excitement, the pupils wide with darkness but lit with the unfamiliar glitter of Issa's familiar haiku.

Is very beautiful, indeed, I thought, knowing that her awkward words were as good as mine at translating such beauty, better really. I thought of our haiku—the losses we found in translation. I thought of the resonant dripping of rain in the mushroom studded woods. I thought of a seventh-century Japanese lover, his robe in a bundle at his feet and his pen in the air, at a loss, alas, for words to match his smile. Looking at the girls laughing in the hall, I smiled too, and thought of Matt and the kimono in with the empty hangers in the closet downstairs.

Tuning Up

When I joined the St. Clare folk choir two years ago the biggest problem was tuning up. On Sunday mornings, Butch took the pitch from a tuning fork, and I tried to match my strings to his—with lots of suggestions from others in the group.

Plink-plunk, our strings said, plink-plunk.

"A little flat," someone would offer as I fiddled with the pegs.

Plunk-plink.

"You think he's flat?" another would chime in.

Eventually our strings matched—plink-plink!—and I would sit back happy for a moment, but only for a moment, because beside me I heard Butch—perfectionist that he is—still fussing with his tuning *after I had finished.* Plink, plunk, plink, plink. The closer he brought his guitar to true pitch the further his tuning drifted from mine. So, while the congregation filed in expectantly, we sat in dread at the front of the chapel—Jennifer, who also plays guitar, Butch, and I—plinking and plunking quietly, perched on the brink of musical mayhem and making matters worse.

"Close enough for folk music," Butch said in despair once, and it soon became our motto. But some Sundays even that excuse wore thin: stuffing our ears with alfalfa wouldn't cure the cacophony our "tuning" produced. Several times the first strum of the opening hymn sounded more like an embarrassing turkey squawk than a chord—bringing winces to the faces of choir and congregation alike.

Eventually, Jennifer came to the rescue with a new battery for her QT 6000 guitar tuner, an electronic device that brings us all to the same pitch, rendering irrelevant the tuning fork and the comments of friends. Now the only enemy is our own fastidiousness because Butch and I still can't resist tuning by ear between songs, sounding harmonics to check our strings as the church service progresses. Obeying separate deities, we follow a gentle jangle into dissonance, hoping that it is good enough for folk music—and a forgiving God.

Harmonics are God's pitches—perfect for tuning during a sermon. They can be played softly so that only the guitarist with an ear to the rosewood body of the instrument can hear them. Sounded by a light touch on a plucked string, harmonics sustain a bell-like ring, the note sounding long enough for another ringing string to be tuned to it. The consonance is deeply pleasing, the guitarist's frown inevitably shifting to a beatific smile when harmonics match—no QT 6000 tuner can create the feeling. Like a perfect carpentry joint, the rising breath of lovers, or a total eclipse of the sun, two become one when harmonics ring true—and the universe lines up behind God.

The fascination with harmonics is as ancient as Pythagoras, the Greek philosopher who first explained them. According to legend, the insight came when he struck a monochord, a single-stringed instrument. Touching the string at the halfway point created an octave jump in sound, and other ratios made musical fourths and fifths—in short, harmonics. All is number, Pythagoras declared when he discovered that these ratios always held true. Reason as well as rhyme govern the heavens, mathematics being the secret and music the clue. The universe, at least, was in tune.

Eventually Pythagoras created a cosmology based on music, arguing that the planets danced in enormous circles according to the same principles as musical harmony. The mechanism for moving these huge, heavenly bodies necessarily produces creaking and scraping, he thought, a music of the spheres. Accustomed to these celestial sounds from birth, humans don't notice the rumblings. We are, to use the Aristotelian explanation, like the coppersmith who no longer hears the ringing hammer strokes of other smithies, the clanking "indistinguishable from its contrary silence." Only when we play music do our dulled ears hear the sounds afresh, the harmonies of our instruments and voices rendering audible, again, the white noise of God.

Once sounded, a harmonic seems to ring forever on airy nothingness, but music is not as spiritual as harmonics—and Pythagoras—make it seem. The mathematics of music fails to acknowledge the physical dimension: catgut, rosewood, and spittle. Music soothes the savage beast, yes, and restores the soul, but it does so by returning the spirit to the battered body.

The obligation of music to the physical world is written on our instruments. My guitar bears the scrapes and scratches of every missed downstroke over the last thirty years as well as the dings and dents of doorjambs, chairbacks, and tabletops that I haven't missed along the way. For my part, I have worn, all my adult life, the callouses at fingertips that metal strings leave to me. It is a kind of communion, this sharing of scars, the toll of the spirit on the body.

My friends exchange licks with their instruments, as well. A double bass is a boxing match—so are the drums—and a guitarist wrestles with a twelve string. Flutes and penny whistles, stashed promiscuously in a canvas sack, look loveable with a ding or two. Blocks, scrapers, cymbals, and clackers travel in the whistle bag, too, clattering like a broken epicycle on the seventh circle of the heavens. Our latest addition, the psaltery, is a pretty box that sits in the lap like a baby, the strings sounded by a horsehair bow. It begs to be handled, and few can resist holding it on their knees and giving it a tickle or two.

Of course, people make music, not wood, steel, and hide. Working jobs all week with little more than a whistle on their lips, they sing and play music for God on Sunday. Jennifer has the perfect folksinger's voice, pretty and hardy at once like wildflowers, and Rachel, on bass, thumps out the heartbeat of the tune. Butch can, it is true, get lost looking for his sheet music and tunes as much as he sings, but once started he is so deeply involved in the song and its meaning that the rest of us are ashamed. Don, drummer and spokesman for the group, cannot help praising us—regardless of the facts—meaning everything he says. And Mindy, our songbird and child, chimes in with a soprano—part laughter, part weeping that is apt, in the middle of a descant, to splinter, joyously, into harmonious giggles.

Usually she is laughing at me, the bungler of the group. I'm opening my prayer book when I should be in the hymnal and still turning the pages of the hymnal while the rest of the choir is into the second score. Once I stood to sing and knocked Mindy's choir stand onto the floor. Another time, my glasses caught on my guitar strap and, popping off my face, flew one aisle back and fell into Don's lap. I'm most myself when I compound the error of late entrances by blundering in in the wrong key, arriving amid God's smithies like a hardhat with a pneumatic drill. On those occasions, even Pythagoras no doubt wonders what in hell has happened to the heavens, the blood rushing to my cheeks a reminder that the music that governs the heavenly bodies is never far from our clumsy, earthly ones either.

"I'm an ecclesiastical folk artist," I joke, as a way of disarming my more cynical friends. Church guitar is, after all, an odd hobby for a middle-aged, heterodox English teacher. I have always believed that people standing and singing while playing the guitar look faintly ridiculous. There is a cover of one of my Huddie Ledbetter albums that shows Leadbelly himself standing ill at ease before a respectable white audience. Wearing a suit with a guitar strapped over it, the old master of the twelve-bar blues—a man capable of murder as well as powerful music—has been reduced to looking like Buckwheat at a talent contest. Why do I do this, I wonder when I stand before the congregation, strap the guitar to my otherwise conventional self, and have the Huddie Ledbetter moment?

Why *do* I do this, I ask myself on Sunday mornings when I rise ahead of the rest of the family and lug my guitar to church in front of God and the world? Sometimes I get so nervous and befuddled in a service that I can't read the words to the song. Once, replacing Butch for a Sunday, I sat in the lead chair, which was particularly distressing because I discovered too late that the congregation took the cues from me. When I sang the wrong score, in *three* verses of one song, half of the congregation followed me into error while the rest created cacophony by singing the right line. Why, oh why, I asked myself on that day, do I *do* this?

Ancient Celts, I've read, used the softening effects of music to stop battles and fortify their better selves, the lances and swords of fighters set aside temporarily as songs were exchanged. Bards would "throw themselves between contending parties, and pacify them, as one by magic subdues the wild beast," Diodorus Siculus, the Greek, writes in a passage on Celtic warfare. I picture a clearing surrounded by old-world trees, and the harp, tuned to bird sounds and howling wind, echoing in the valley, reminding warriors of life and loss. I think of our wooden flute, which sounds like women weeping when Mindy plays. Even among the barbarians, the Greek writer Siculus concludes, music tames savagery and "frenzy yields to wisdom."

There comes a moment somewhere in our Sunday songs when that particular kind of yielding takes place, and I know after all why I, clumsy as I am, do this. Eventually, inevitably, and in the midst of my confusion, I find the right note, shed the bewildering anxiety of being me, and for the length of a tune, perhaps, I am us. Like barbarians on a battleground, my neighbors and I meet over a song and walk away without exchanging a blow. Unlike solitary arts such as writing, singing is communal, with the chorus blending differences at the meeting place of a chord. When I sing, I find my voice among other voices and like Celtic warriors at rest give in, without surrendering, to something larger and better than myself. "Frenzy," as the Greek put it, "yields"—and we all come away a little wiser.

St. Clare's choir was not begun for the lofty purpose of my salvation. It was born out of necessity. More than ten years ago the church was a mountain mission with no organist or piano player in the congregation. Butch and Jennifer *were* the choir, playing, Jennifer told me once, the same three songs over and over. They met in an abandoned Methodist chapel at the end of a dirt road in the middle of the woods, a beautiful place. I first heard them there more than five years ago, in autumn, the church windows filled with red and yellow leaves, the choir making a heavenly jangle of simple songs about giving and sharing and loving—doing the Lord's chores and nothing more.

Unfortunately, we are not always up to singing God's songs. Our choir only practices one night a week—at my place usually, the chairs in a circle in the downstairs den—and that evening has to be squeezed into busy lives. Jennifer and Don own and run a candy company, Mindy sells real estate, and Butch builds houses. I've seen Butch so exhausted during practice that he fell asleep between songs. The rest of us often come in cross or sore. Music, a barometer of moods, cannot avoid picking up the lows of our day, occasionally making practice a torture for anyone in earshot—God included.

Several months ago the group made a recording, a promotional tool for the church building fund. The studio, located in a small house on a rural highway, serves myriad gospel and country singers in our area and is surprisingly professional, able to record twenty-four tracks from microphones that hear every giggle and sigh.

We gave it our all, arriving giddy in several cars, full of music and jokes and stories. "We're excited!" Don said, as he often does. Unfortunately, we only had one day to do all the recording, and the session dragged on and on, much of it spent getting sound levels, microphones, and, of course, tunings right. The studios were small so Don and Rachel had to play in another room, a violation of the intimacy of the group, which bothered us as well. When it was done, we rode home in a gloomy silence, fingers, voices, and spirits numb.

A month later I saw Mindy at a concert sponsored by my school. It was the week that the tape was released. "It's terrible," she said sadly, "all soupy—something wrong with the mix." Later I listened to the recording myself. Not terrible but not *us* was my verdict. The sensitive mikes had picked up more of our weariness with life than our delight in each other and music. Some changes would have made the recording better—we could have taken two days, for instance—but no amount of time would make the tape sound like us.

We are what the recording cannot pick up and save, the tip of an ancient and fragile art. We extend the living tradition of music-making, which does not try to hold on to songs but passes them on—a shade flat, perhaps, but alive—along an unending string of perishable voices. I have been told that any time music moves from one medium to another—from voice to tape, from tape to disk—some quality of the sound is inevitably sacrificed in the process. What lasts of our singing is not what is captured in a cassette but what is spent on the air, in notes played by instruments that change tune with the weather and never sound the same twice.

God doesn't do encores.

One musical performance unlikely to have an encore any time soon was the singing of Tibetan monks in our Georgia mountain town. Who knows the odd turn of events that brought them our way? But there they were, one Tuesday in October, chanting music thousands of years old from a land halfway around the world. It was too good to miss, so Barbara and I took the kids, after warning them that what they heard and saw would seem strange.

The program notes say that this music is holy, each number the result of a mystical experience millennia ago and preserved in an unbroken oral tradition. The purpose of the music is to heal, to "establish communication with the higher powers of good," and this particular tour was an extension of that ancient ambition by modern-day Tibetans from a culture under threat, an attempt to bring this force for healing and goodness to the rest of the world. It had gotten as far as the auditorium by the blinking stoplight in our town.

It was—believe me—very strange, and at first all I could do was take in the oddity: monks in gaily colored, sleeveless robes singing, chirping, and groaning a music completely lacking in Western harmony or melody. This was chanting so ancient that it sounded like animal noises and seemed directly of the earth—no Pythagorean spheres here, but a rumbling of the machinery.

Oddest of all was the *dung chen* played by Gangkar Tulku, a large, dark-skinned man, youngest of all the singers in appearance but oldest, too, since he, as a child, was recognized as the reincarnation of an ancient high lama from eastern Tibet. His instrument was a magnificent and goofy sounding long-horn trumpet. The American liaison introducing the *dung chen* said that we should brace ourselves because it sounded like the roar of an elephant. After the performance a friend of mine wondered which end of the elephant the man had in mind.

To get past this whirl of sound—to hear the music—I tried to pay attention to what was valued in their performance. Volume, certainly—the grating honk of bass voices resounding, unmiked, through the auditorium. Smoothness, too—an unending, undivided sound, one note gliding into another without customary intervals, or intervals of any kind, and the chanting never stopping, the breathing staggered so that every moment is filled with voice.

Over the centuries, Tibetans have cultivated the art of *jok-kay*, a multiphonic chanting that enables a single monk to sing the three notes of a chord simultaneously, a deep-throated, sustained bellow with barely audible overtones. When all the monks chant this way they make a torrent of sound, "power language" they call it, rocking the auditorium. At times, it sounded like a barnyard. At a loss for an appropriate response to the music, I clung to anything I could recognize. The dancing helped; dithyrambic steps in illustrative garments seemed less unfamiliar and often gave concrete expression to the themes in the songs.

It was not until "Dur-Dak Gar-Cham," though, the "Dance of the Skeleton Lords," that I reclaimed whatever my brain retains of its primordial past and felt the majesty of these performances. Two monks appeared as Cemetery Lords and, dressed as skeletons, danced joyously, representing liberation from the living death created by a slavery to things. In this dance I saw the greatest fear of all humanity, the horror of a life without spirit—a life wasted on things—and heard in a song older than Pythagoras, older than harmony, one of the earliest attempts of human beings to relieve spiritual deadness with music. The lamas, visiting a remote corner of the strange land where I live, were singing for us all.

"I liked it," my ten-year-old son, Sam, said when the performance was over. "It was weird." And it was. I thanked the student sitting to my left for accompanying me during one of the strangest hours of my life—and she laughed. What made the event eerie, though, was that it was not entirely strange; there remained amid the oddity a haunting residue of the familiar. Several days after the performance I leaned my guitar in front of me and, looking into its sound hole, plucked the lowest string. I listened to the long, resonant, continuous moan it made and remembered the monks. I thought of Celtic bards tuning instruments in the midst of bearded savages and spheres with fiery stars and planets bolted to their rims rolling along the tracks of heaven. How long have we filled darkness with music?

The Sunday after the Tibetan performance was the first folk mass since our recording, and before the service I joked about the tape our group had made. "Scotty liked it," I said while we passed the QT 6000 around. Scotty is my parakeet, a discerning but temperamental musician in his own right who sings along with Mozart while inserting his head in the tiny bell in his bird cage. "Halfway through the first number," I told the group, "he put on his bell and started warbling."

To begin the service we sang "As the Deer" for a meditation, a hymn based on Psalm 42, and Mindy played the psaltery with the group for the first time. "Something old, something new"—the essence of folk music. We listened to each other and sang as one, creating a place where the Skeleton Lords of sound drive the worst in us away and the best of ourselves—no matter how feeble that is—finds the best in others. A hush fell on us all when the last chord was struck.

Sometimes I do not participate in communion at our church. Often I feel nothing during the ceremony, and sometimes my life is such a mess that, regardless of theological assurances, I simply do not feel forgivable. This Sunday, though, I decided to join in.

Butch, as usual, opened a space in the grove of music stands, and I followed him.

When we go to communion, we leave our instruments behind. They look so forlorn there, stacked on the floor or leaning against chairback and stand, like kids left out at snack time, while we stand silent and contrite at God's table with cupped and empty hands. When the feast is done, we return to guitar, whistle, and cymbal. We strap them to our bodies, bringing them to hand and mouth and lap. They plink and plunk, happy to see us again, it seems, and we silence them sternly. We look into each other's eyes to be sure we are ready. At last Butch strikes a chord—frenzy yields—and we find our voices in an enormous and unending choir of the spirit. In tune, indeed, we sing.

The Phantom Lover

Even though I am white, and my background is Anglo-Saxon and Protestant, I may be a member of the smallest minority in America: I don't own a TV. Daily I'm made aware of my minority status by all the unfamiliar faces of stars on the glossy covers of magazines, and I often find myself pretending to laugh at jokes I don't get because I'm not up on *Cheers* or *Twin Peaks* or *David Letterman.* All this is by choice though not everyone believes it. "Those poor things," one of the workers in my building said about my family and me when she learned that we didn't own a set. "Can't somebody buy one for them?" The answer, I have come to understand in the years that I have lived outside the flickering glow of the cathode ray tube, is no. A TV in my house would be too expensive, no matter what the cost.

It was not always this way. Once, in the early years of my marriage, I used most of a box of aluminum foil in a failed attempt to improve reception and pick up—I'm ashamed to admit—the *Mary Tyler Moore Show.* At first I simply added to the mouse ears, which did little more than give us a tantalizing, fuzzy outline of our pert heroine, so in desperation, I unloaded the box and crawled out the window, extending the antenna into the yard and moving about from bush to bush, all the while yelling "is it better *now?*" to my wife inside.

"No," Barbara said at last while I waited at the end of my tinsel tether, "but for a second there I think we picked up Radio Free Europe."

I was a TV kid myself, my preadolescent days taken up by *My Three Sons, Leave It to Beaver,* and *Gunsmoke.* If the show was a favorite, like *Maverick,* the whole family watched, my dad with cigarettes and a lighter in a tidy stack on the coffee table in front of him, my mother and sister under afghans, their feet propped beside them on the couch, and my brother and I on the floor—all of us lulled into a jittery stupor. I also remember other nights on my stomach on the rug, head propped on fists, looking up into the box of light, the house empty except for me and the laugh track.

Some of my earliest memories are linked with television. I can recall sitting at a TV tray during lunch watching noon-time shows and eating peanut butter and mayonnaise sandwiches (a wretched thought), chips, and Hostess Cupcakes. Suddenly, a character popped onto the screen saying "pluck your magic twanger froggie—hi kids, hi, hi, hi, hi, hi," while a big spring went boing in the background. No wonder I'm a maniac! The rest of my lunchtime viewing is, mercifully, a blur, but I do remember that the sandwich was sweet and the cupcakes, cut in half on the plate, exposing twin white hearts, were never as perfect as the ones that I saw in the ads.

In college, it is true, I did not watch much television except for Sunday nights when my gang gathered around a set for a camp viewing of *The Wild, Wild West.* By then TV had become little more than an ironic interlude between a day of studies and a night on the town, and we spent most of our time making fun of the show, laughing when a foolish character named Artemus Gordon came on. Artemus Gor-*done* we shouted, cracking up like fools ourselves.

I rejoined the ranks of serious viewers—as did most of my generation—with the Watergate Hearings. I worked at a construction job on Martha's Vineyard, and I watched the big events from a local bar during breaks. It was odd living among Yanks again after having gone to a North Carolina college. And the oddity was reinforced by the face of Sam Ervin on TV each day, the old Tarheel bringing the president to his knees. Most of the viewing that summer was simply good theater, the story of a hero defeated by his own tragically flawed character, as John Dean, the bureaucrat with the prodigious memory who was not much older than we, told all, his pretty wife beside him, cold and silent as a porcelain doll. Watergate culminated in Nixon's stiff-armed farewell from Air Force One, and clearly by the time it was over I was hooked again, ready to take my place on the couch of American life. It was not long after that, having returned to Charlotte, North Carolina, with my wife that I, hungry for a sitcom, was hanging out of the window of our duplex stringing aluminum foil into the next county.

TV is magical, not simply because images appear—presto!—in our living rooms, but because of the eerie nature of those disembodied apparitions. Inviting in their insubstantiality and somnolently seductive, they are as delightful and empty as a dinner of desserts. I have fond memories of watching *Sesame Street* with my infant son before we packed up the TV. I remember the summer day when the screen first caught his attention. He held his hand out to shapes—Big Bird and Ernie—that were no longer just a jumble of colors and not yet identifiable characters to his one-year-old mind. He tried to talk to them, though he could not talk, and looked with growing curiosity as the shape kept talking back. He was, in short, into it, making the leap from what little he knew of reality to the shapes on the screen by participating in the medium.

Marshall McLuhan long ago pointed out that TV images—created out of thousands of discrete dots—implicated viewers, folded them into the process of watching by inviting them into a gossamer web of negative space, a mesh of sights at least half of their own making. Our mind connects the dots, lending depth and perspective, and ultimately, meaning to the electronic *trompe l'oeil* of the tube. And yet, the experience sedates us, engaging just enough of our senses to lull us into a stupor. It is, McLuhan wrote, a cool medium. We sit mesmerized, our perceptions of a lit square heightened as our imagination is dulled, and many remain locked in this self-imposed trance until the test pattern comes squealing on the screen.

Not long after Matt crawled out of my lap and began to totter upright, we moved to a remote area of the southern Appalachian Mountains. TV reception there was bad; the signal in our cozy valley had to be boosted by a system of mountaintop transmitters, and houses were equipped with serious antennas. My aluminum foil days were over. It was, in fact, the beginning of the end of TV for us. In Charlotte when the TV broke we got it repaired immediately, and once, when it took an electrical hit on a stormy Sunday morning, I paid triple the price to have it fixed in time for . . . oh, for *some*thing. But when the TV broke at our mountain home—the closest repair shop several hours away—we gave up on the fuzzy picture and stored the old set in the garage between a lawn mower and a stack of newspapers where, for years, like Cyclops, it cast a blind eye on darkness. Our TV days were done.

We deprive ourselves in no other way. We own cars, a CD player, an excellent radio and sound system, and were among the first to get a computer—a vintage TRS-80 that I still use. Five years ago—after more than a decade with no electronic images in the house—we compromised and bought a VCR and a computer monitor to watch videos, but still no cable, no CNN, and no network.

There is a loss here. I miss seeing weather on TV, since one glance at a map tells me more than all the jabber on the radio about barometric pressure and intermittent precipitation. Baseball on the radio may be fine—the medium ideally suited to the luxuriously slow pace of the game—but I need a TV to watch basketball, which on the radio is little more than an auditory blur of names and fouls. So when NCAA March Madness hits, I become a pest, inviting myself over to friends' houses, bearing gifts in six-packs.

Barbara's father frankly worried about our children growing up in a house without television. A believer in progress, he thought that the kids would be placed at a disadvantage in a world that, for good or ill, is fueled by the information on TV. In a way he was right, and I am saddened at times when I think of my kids trying valiantly to appear in-the-know among their friends at school, every one a devotee of the small screen. There is a residual sense of not being with it, or for that matter, not being American, if you don't own a TV. My kids don't miss television—they never had it—but they have become sleuths of cultural information, figuring out fashions, lunch-table allusions, and even basic product information by piecing together bits of conversations. That has been hard on them, I know. For years after we stuffed the set in the garage, my son—embarrassed—would tell his friends at school that we had a TV but it was broken.

One consolation is the TV vacation. This week my daughters and I took a trip to see my son at college—the same son who had once sat on my lap to watch Big Bird. The drive takes ten hours, and we filled the time with show tunes, miles and miles of singing and laughing and growing sentimental. But when we arrived at the motel, beat and bleary eyed, the first thing we did was plop the suitcases on the floor, stretch out on the motel bed, and turn on the TV.

Most parents, I suspect, tell the kids to turn off the motel television set—"You can watch that at home!" they say—but our kids can't, and neither can we, so we indulge them and ourselves, watching the tube while St. Louis, or Charleston, or in this case, Charlottesville, happens without us, just beyond the peephole of our door.

After years of going cold turkey, a couple of hours of TV can be disorienting. I get an eerie sense that I'm not myself and have become, instead, a titillated consumer. Unlike most viewers, I can't easily distinguish songs on MTV from the commercials and begin to wonder, when I come across in-depth reports on the latest films or sneakers fads or advances at Microsoft, if anyone can tell where advertising ends and TV begins. It is all one big infomercial. Cars, stereos, computers, and beautiful bodies—not to mention pizza, beer, salsa, and chips—parade across the screen, creating God knows what desires in me. In the convenience store down the street from the motel I have an uncontrollable urge to buy a Yoo Hoo and deodorant in a tube and find my eyes taking in a teeny bopper with legs as long as Italy, a waiflike, pucker-faced imitation of countless models from my afternoon viewing. Sheesh!

The O.J. Simpson trial was in the news on this trip, and I noticed the unreality of it all. We ate pizza and cracked jokes while Nicole Simpson's sister took the stand and wept through a clip—wrinkled brow, mouth torn open with sadness and pulled down at the corners in nervousness and grief, the voice unable to complete a sentence without body-wracking, uncontrollable crying.

Alice, my nine-year-old, who is deeply affected when anyone cries, sat on the bed wide-eyed and bewildered—a breadstick in her hand—trying to take in the testimony. Simpson, the witness told us between sobs, picked Nicole up during one fight, "threw her against the wall" and "out of the house," where she "ended up falling on her elbows and her butt." Another time he grabbed her crotch and said, "This is where babies come from and this belongs to me." I got up and changed the channel, but not, judging from my girl's downcast eyes, before some damage was done. Later, the clip was repeated on *Entertainment Tonight*, the late-night network, and local news, and I guess, every hour on the hour on CNN.

We had taken the trip to Charlottesville in part to let my older daughter, a senior in high school, see the university. I had gone to school there myself, and her brother was now enrolled. Interested in foreign language, she visited a French class and the French House while Alice and I took in Monticello. "Thomas Jefferson was fond of gadgets," the guide explained, noting his interest in the latest technology of his time as we stood before a large clock that told the minute, hour, and day of the week by means of suspended weights that went through the floor and into the basement. "Were Mr. Jefferson alive today," she added, "he would, no doubt, own a computer and a wide-screen TV."

No doubt.

We were also in town to see a basketball game in the Coliseum across from our motel. The Cavaliers, on a hot streak, had won the last five or six games in a row, most in overtime. Now they faced the Seminoles from Florida State. After so many close calls, the announcer of the pregame show suggested that officials warn the elderly and those who had a heart condition to stay away. The game lived up to its billing—a "nail-biter," one announcer said later—the contest ending in yet another glorious overtime victory for Virginia.

As we walked to the game at the Coliseum, a gentle snow began to fall, and I found myself thinking of the ways basketball has helped Matt and me stay close despite the miles between us. Each home victory he calls, knowing that he can bring the news to me first, describing highlights that I miss without a TV. And of course there was *this*, the game that I come to see each year. Matt sat with the students in a different section, but I had the girls, and he visited with us before the game started as well as at the half, telling us which players to watch.

I sat next to other alums, and the woman beside me, in her fifties I'd say, with bobbed red hair and a professorial look, knew every player and kept a running commentary going. She and I laughed at the gaudy warm-up suits of the Seminoles. "Florida," I said, archly. But irony soon gave way to less subtle commentary when the official made a bad call, and she joined some of the fans in throwing her box of popcorn on the court. We picked up a technical for that one, a sacrifice well worth the price of audience participation, she told me. "What a show-off," she screamed when our star player went behind his back with the ball and attempted to drive for the basket. "He thinks he can dribble," she shouted as he lost control and committed a turnover. "None of these guys can dribble," she confided to me in a stage whisper, as the opponent took an easy lay-up at the other end of the court. She was getting pretty worked up. When we got the ball back and our flashy guard once again began to bring it down court, she was on her feet, chanting "don't dribble, don't dribble," an odd but irresistible little cheer. Soon several of us joined in, and I wondered, looking down at the balding tops of expert television announcers below, if any of them were making such a trenchant analysis of the moment.

That evening we relived the victory by watching the highlights on TV, the game reduced to a thirty-second clip that was amazingly thorough, since it took time for shots of cheerleaders and crazy fans as well as the six or seven great plays of the game. In less than a minute I watched the images that only edited TV can produce—scenes of extraordinary agility selected from various times in the game and spliced together to give the illusion of constant excitement, continual grace, the ball ripping through the net in rapid succession. Even the steal that enraged the fan beside me was there, though our little chant on the dangers of dribbling was inaudible in all the ruckus.

We spent most of the clip looking for ourselves, of course—but without success—and I realized afterward that even if I had found my face, I would never have located me: the afterglow of Monticello and bits and snatches of French with my daughters and happy thoughts of my son—all that, the private nature of public events, is inevitably lost to the eye of the camera. We may have seen our images but would have missed ourselves. When the local sports news was over, the image of the crying woman returned to the screen to tell the story of her poor sister's crotch yet again, and I had to hunt through most of the stations before I could get her testimony out of the room.

After a few days at the tube, I found that I had turned doughy and dopey and on the morning we were scheduled to leave Charlottesville I crawled out of a motel bed of nachos with a gauzy head and complete dyspepsia of body and soul, and watched more weeping on the morning news. It was time to go home.

Our days spin out differently when we don't watch TV—words and flesh, not images, at the core of our lives—and in this way the day-to-day experience in my house is different from that of most Americans. All weekend in Charlottesville there had been television reports of snow—dire warnings that we could get four or five feet of it—and I was beginning to worry that we would have to extend our trip to TV-land by a week. But most of the snow went north of us; we saw it all on the local news—random images of shovels, spinning tires, and bundled bodies in a dizzying, white Pennsylvania landscape. "Looks like we dodged the bullet this time," the Charlottesville announcer said, cheerily. The trip home was long and uneventful—the same old songs—and by late afternoon we were home, dumping suitcases in the living room and passing out hugs. Pictures of Monticello made the rounds, as did a book on cartooning for Sam and a Virginia sweatshirt for Barbara. Barbara had the fire going in the fireplace when we arrived, and by ten we had settled into easy chairs and were talking and reading, as usual.

It is true that we read a good deal in our house, the words in books and magazines liberating us from the images that are transmitted at the speed of light through our culture. Media images deplete the imagination of alternatives, so that Daisy in *The Great Gatsby* becomes Mia Farrow, or whoever, for all who see the movie, while Daisy in the book fills with the text-altered image of every reader's unrequited love. No sooner does the TV plop us down on our couches than it lifts us out of the house as well, beaming us, with or without Scotty, up and away, but when books take us on journeys they bring us, inevitably, home.

When Barbara and I put the books down, our journeys turn literal and local since we often fill up our evenings by walking, taking our world in strides, the familiar concrete paths offering up each night a different scene, one without plot or manipulation, one that simply is. Strolling through a landscape puts our lives into a perspective missing in books, the scenery appropriating us in the act of our taking it in, our bodies now seen in relation to the people, animals, plants, and objects of that world, even if we do not touch them. Landmarks become familiar—the swings at the Mayor's Park, the pastel houses along Maple Street, the gazebo hidden under oaks, and the mountain vista that it offers up, effortlessly, each day.

It's the call of a larger world—not the international one transmitted in the airwaves, no, one larger than that. We do not steal these sights and sounds when Barbara tugs the sleeve of my coat and says "look!"—we become a part of it all. When walking is done, we talk, our words warmed by breath. The vagaries of conversation hold us—the absence of a script, the silences, the verbal ramble that makes a good talk like a good walk. "Did you get the brakes checked" becomes, by turns as intricate and mysterious as a curled flame, the words "love" and "yes."

Does TV mesmerize us in the same way that a fire does? I doubt it. The fire does not distract, though the elaborate pattern of leaping flames delights; rather, it leaves us in a meditative state—no catharsis but a resonant image that reflected in our eyes finds an analogy in the flickering consummation of our day and of our days. It says *live!*—in part because its embers teach lessons about dying. When I poke the fire or look out the window at the snow, no one is selling me anything, and I shed my consumer self, all my borrowed wants, feeling the tug of desires closer to home, aware of my own animal nature. I hear my breath, not the amplified breathing of others, and know better who I am because I know what I want.

I understand that these desires, simple as they appear, come from somewhere—something in my past—and images from TV are part of that. Wasn't there always a fire at the hearth of the Ponderosa, Adam, Little Joe, and Hoss—as well as silver-haired Ben—all stepping away from its comfortable flames, spurs jangling, cradling a hot cup of who-knows-what as their eyes filled with the possibilities of this week's adventure? How many presidents lied to us on television, a crackling fire in the background lulling us into acquiescence? I don't escape the influences of my society or my past, but I do find them to be transformed by a house free of TV. Desires, mulled over and sifted, have time and silence to develop in me. Assimilating with lifelong needs, drives, and urges, they are less artificially achieved than they would be in a television household, the thirst that brings the glass to my hand beginning at my lips rather than my eyes.

Even sex is different, in part because television uses sex to sell, both obviously and subliminally—an electronic pimp to all in its chalky glare. Our hand falls to our lover's body differently in a TV culture where we satisfy desires created by the body on screen, not by the body in the room. Turning to the body beside us as a surrogate, all of us—including the person behind the image on TV—suffer by the comparison, I'm sure. I may come to accept that the peanut butter sandwiches and cupcakes I ate while watching TV as a child were delivered to me in ads, but what about the wife in my arms?

In the absence of TV it is the glance across the room that catches the eye, the hand on our thigh that raises expectations—expectations that that glance and that hand alone can fulfill completely. Phantom lovers fall away. Some day when Barbara and I are alone we may get a TV—who knows?—but for now at least it is truly broken in us, a wafer delivering us to ourselves and each other, restoring the rough and mighty feel of flesh to our hands.

Home(less)

Fuzzy with early morning, I stand in the middle of the living room in my mountain home, staring at the picture window. It glowers back, ebony, only a hint of dawn's red horizon line running through it. The reflection of a face floats there, muffin-puffy and gouged with shadows.

Sounds emerge: the padding of my daughter's slippers across wood floors, thonk of a dropped hairbrush, the dog's whine from the basement, muffled sounds of perfunctory "g'mornings," peppery clatter of a box of barrettes scattered on linoleum, the thud-umpf, thud-umpf when one son body-slams a brother and the brother socks back. I hear the creak of doors and the gurgle of a sink. Radios send up separate stations in brilliant cacophony. Sam appears wide-eyed at the top of the landing and crows, "aaah . . . what's up doc?" There's a scream, a cry, a squeal, a groan. . . .

Soon enough I am brought to myself by the house waking up around me, the face at the window replaced by the light of day and a crisp, winter morning.

(As temperatures dropped below freezing last night, Atlanta's shelters filled to overflowing and a grim seasonal ritual began.)

First frost speckles the window edge and coats the handrails in glitter. It sparkles in the air and blanches the lawn. It tumbles stalks and blackens blooms.

"Where's the sugar, Dad?" Sam says, tugging at my pajamas, a box of cereal under his arm.

(Police took about eight men to the Salvation Army's shelter, 400 Luckie Street, according to the lodge manager. He said police normally bring only one or two men a week. . . .)

When we get dressed in the morning we stand before closets or mirrors or bare walls, looking out while being in. We are shy, unwilling to face the world until we can face each other, unwilling to face each other until we are ready to take on the world. Nessa stands at a mirror with a hot comb, trying on different expressions. Matt, at another mirror, brushes around his braces and frowns. I button up my shirt, looking slackfaced into a thicket of hangers, reluctant to dispel the last wisps of nighttime dreaminess.

The house shelters us, first from the world and then from each other. It has corners and nooks, locked rooms and closets, a basement study and a spooky attic. It gives us hiding places where we can be ourselves, and in the mornings we seek them out. Clustered within walls but lost to all but ourselves, we turn up the volume of our radios (drink deeply of crime, despair, and homelessness) and drown out the ones we love.

(At the Atlanta union mission homeless men slept in the chapel after all the beds were filled. "We had a full house," the desk manager said.)

Full house — that's the way it feels early in the morning all of us trying to get out at once. Matt carries a bowl in one hand and a cereal box in another. He opens the refrigerator with his foot. Sam strolls in and pops him in the stomach. Nessa rummages through the pantry. "Where's the sugar?" she growls, her hair in rollers the size of beer cans.

"What kind of reception do you get with those," I say to exasperate her, tweaking the radio knob of her ear.

"*Dad*dy" she groans, "where *is* the sugar?" She scrutinizes me. A lost cause, she thinks. I'll get nowhere with this boob. She cocks an eyebrow.

"Where's Mom?"

Alice pads in clutching two stuffed rabbits. "I'm thirsty," she announces, leaning her bunnies against each other on the table in front of her.

Full house. A house full of *us*, I think, but it's not true. Beyond the fluorescent glow of the kitchen, dark corners of the house remain asleep, lit by a radio dial or a needle of sunlight through curtains, bathed in our absence, a generous emptiness of corners and shadows and bookcases and bureau tops all waiting, set against the far-off clatter of our antics.

In one room Barbara, the mother of these children, sleeps with the covers over her head.

(Residents can get coffee and doughnuts and, occasionally, soup. The director said the shelter could always use donations of "coffee, creamer, and disinfectant.")

Morning light: glittering glasses cast frail spectra on floor, ceiling, and door. Breakfast dishes scrubbed and set in the drainer gleam, waiting at a quiet stop in a routine that carries them from drainer to cupboard to table to sink.

At home, the world submits to our patterns. We smooth the bindings of books with our palms, line up jars along the counter, get the fork in with the forks. "I know it's here, somewhere," we say, our losses relegated to irritations.

These are the comforts of routine. We reach back for the book on the shelf where we left it, and the shelf is there even if the book is not. And if the book is not, a hole is left where it belongs, the other books on the shelf leaning in loving consort toward this absence.

(disinfectant . . . coffee . . . disinfectant . . . creamer . . . disinfectant . . . doughnuts . . . disinfectant . . .)

Clean sheets—all that billowy white! It is Tuesday morning, and Barbara takes the squared-off bundles out of the linen closet and goes from room to room changing beds. A radio babbles in the background (". . . on a routine patrol the police took more than thirty men to shelters in the hours before snow. . . ."), but she hums a tune to herself and hardly hears. Like a magician she throws her hands high in the air, and the white bundle opens and unfurls in front of her—spreading a sugary fluff overhead at her command (". . . in the hours before snow and sleet hit. . . .").

Home is the place for simple extravagances; the abracadabra of everyday.

Barbara spreads her body across the bed, tucking in sheet corners, and when she has finished rolls over and looks at the ceiling, recovering some part of her soul in the magic of a moment wasted. ("On routine patrol . . . sleet hit . . . city Thursday, thirty men . . . to shelters, according to . . . took more than . . . Atlanta police officers. . . .") She opens her arms, the bed white and clean beneath her, and smiles for no one to see.

("The space for thirty men goes quickly," a police spokesman said.)

A clear, crisp winter day—that is the scene in the picture window. The chill in the air makes the sky look crisp and bright.

"Water drops have a prismatic effect," my older son says. "They scatter light. Ice crystals let light pass through."

Sounds good, I think, sipping coffee and looking out over the lawn. An icy shimmer. A sharp chill. Razors slicing deep into the day.

(And on the horizon, clouds.)

(The state's earliest freeze was recorded October 11, 1906. Its latest freeze was December 8, 1931. The latest first freeze in recent years was December 2, 1985.)

Dust finds the unused spaces in a house. Composed, in part, of our skin, which flakes off even while we sleep, it rises into the air when we strip beds or shake out the laundry. Dead leavings float through the house, settling on the spots we do not use. We fill vacuums with our residue, sweeping out corners diligently, but our dust always returns. If we could silence the hum of the house, and the thumps and clonkings of our clumsy selves, if we could pull the plug on the machinery of our lives, this whispering hiss of falling dust would remain to haunt us. Death is always at home with us, piling up in corners of the places we feel safe.

("The shelter could use more towels and linens," the desk managers said. "The necessities. . . .")

. . . the superfluous: a lamp left on in an empty room casting an eerie light that no one sees, lounge chairs puffed with our absence but bearing the sagging imprint of past use, dry and gleaming sinks, a framed watercolor so familiar no one sees its daily announcements in yellows, pinks, and blues, a locked trunk, a stack of games we've outgrown, a red *Monopoly* hotel tucked into the carpet edge out of reach of the vacuum, one half of a recorder in a box, magnifying glasses with cloudy lenses, plastic trophies, dead batteries rolling in the sock drawer, and books read long ago, the bindings having become old, old friends.

In houses unused things wait on us. They collect our dust.

(A spokesperson for the facility said the gym can house fifty to seventy-five people, and the corps youth hall can hold another thirty-five to fifty.)

During the afternoon hours when it is empty a house changes mood, and all is shaded in sepia. Released of us, it becomes a thing again, as undefiled as an oak. It is the snake's skin rubbed off in a crack between the rocks. It is a styrofoam cup flipped out of the car window and tumbling down an embankment where it is to wait out its millennium neglected.

A house is patient when it is empty, letting the day clown and carry on around it, remaining unresponsive and empty-eyed like a doll.

(A few days before last autumn's first freeze, concern rose for the homeless left in the cold after two transient men were found dead, both from a combination of exposure and alcohol.)

"Anybody home?"

Flipping on lights and opening curtains, we drive the sepia away. Shadows lift out of corners with a dull flapping and begin their nocturnal rounds. We bang around, setting groceries on the counter and tossing sneakers in the chair.

We do not hear the burrower under the porch, or the scavenger behind the molding, the owners of the empty house, but they wait on us just as the empty house waits on us and will outlast us all.

("The men come in the early afternoon and hide on the steps out of the wind," a police spokesman said. "Every night there are more.")

What do you do with a porch in the winter? Snow settles on the rails and, blown by icy winds, drifts into corners. The charcoal cooker wears tufts of snow in its handles. Water freezes in the dog's dish.

In the winter our porches go to the dogs. Bundled up we rush past the creaking swing without lifting our faces from our scarves. Propping a grocery bag on one knee, we fumble for a key, shivering. The dog and cat, curled up with each other to keep warm, lift their eyes to watch us.

("We need to get these people off the streets," the director of one downtown shelter said after returning from a grocery excursion laden with eggs, cereal, hamburger meat, and the like. "We've got enough to last for a couple of days.")

Bags fill the counter tops and the kitchen table. Gallon milk containers stand cold and chaste at the counter's end. Kids mill around.

Nessa, telling some long story about lunch at school, gives the bags a desultory examination. Sam hides cookies. Alice hangs on to her two bunnies and watches us all.

Loading the refrigerator until racks are full, Barbara has to rearrange things. Matt flips cans to me, and I put them on the shelves, passing the common wealth of our lives from one set of hands to another, anticipating the oreo-hostess-hershey's-breyers-little debbie delights to come.

"Hey look!" says Nessa, interrupting her monologue. "Sugar!"

(The shelter always needs towels, coffee, and sugar. "We don't care if towels are used, we wash everything.")

Abundance . . . and garbage. We keep trash in the basement in large plastic bags. The pile begins in front of the workbench and lines the wall beside the back door. Bags fill silently and unobtrusively, accumulating like the days of our lives (in the shadow of our lives). At the end of the week we tag them and haul them off to the dump, sweeping the floor bare again.

(In the shadow of our lives . . .)

In a circle of light from the table lamp, Sam reads Aesop's *Fables* to me and Alice before he goes to bed.

"No," said the Fox to the Lion. "I will not go into your cave."

Sam clips his words and speaks in the lilting monotone of children reading. "'On the ground I see many marks of animals that have gone in,' says the Fox, 'but nowhere do I see marks of animals that have come out. . . .'"

He pushes his hair back from his forehead and clonks shoes together in rhythm to the words. Alice and her bunnies—all wide-eyed—look on with varying degrees of comprehension. I look out the gloomy window—the storm is coming. Beasts (susceptible to the elements) search out lairs, and the dog scratches at the door.

(In the shelter of our lives . . .)

Once I found a rat groggy with poison tottering in our hall. I covered it with a towel and beat it with a hammer until it quit squirming.

(The shelter always needs . . . we don't care if the towels are . . . if we run across someone who is . . . we don't care . . . susceptible to the elements . . . we're not out there searching . . . every night there are more . . . on the steps out of the wind . . .) until it quit squirming . . . (towels, coffee, and sugar . . .) "Hey look! Sugar!" . . .

(disinfectant . . . we're running low . . . we wash . . . those who are susceptible to . . . we wash everything . . .)

I line the fireplace grille with newspapers tied in knots and then lay in a bed of twigs. I load in the wood next, sticks the size of my little finger first. I begin small, working my way up to logs, laying the sticks first one way and then another until I've used up my bundle. One match and —*poof*— the whole pile goes, the smoke drawn by flames up the flue, out of the house.

All circle round, eyes dotted red.

(As long as it's as cold as it was last night, it's an emergency. We don't turn them away.)

In the hours between eight and ten, after the dinner dishes have been cleared, and the little kids have gone down for the night, then we hear it: the creak at the pantry, the whoosh of the refrigerator door.

Snitching: the game of stealing food, one bite at a time. Here the gift of easy access and the art of nonchalance meet.

Nessa opens the closet to toss an empty pen refill in the trash and emerges with potato chips on her breath. Matt sidles through the kitchen and exits chewing.

Fingers slip into bags, rake the peanut butter lid or, moistened, find the purer joys of the sugar jar—and make their inevitable, unsanitary way into the mouth.

The endless dessert: snitching.

(coffee . . . disinfectant . . . creamer . . . disinfectant . . . doughnuts . . . disinfectant . . . sugar)

The storm hits at night, the wind whipping through pinetops and stripping the remaining leaves from oaks. All around us the woods creak.

By nightfall the wind roars down the mountain. I stop on the way to the woodpile to listen and watch, holding my hat on my head. The edge of the woods glows from the yellow houselights, the trees bobbing in a drunken dance. I shiver and go inside.

(The shelter filled its 122 beds at about 11 P.M. said a clerk monitoring incoming homeless people. "We're well over capacity," he said. "We're nervous.")

The dog scratches at the door . . .

("Every night there are more," he said.)

The dog scratches at the door . . .

(We're nervous . . . we're well over capacity . . . we're nervous . . . every night there are more . . . we're nervous . . . every night . . .)

The dog scratches at the door . . .

(We're nervous.)

. . . and I let her in.

("An estimated seven to twelve thousand homeless people live in the Atlanta area, and there are 3,200 beds at sixty-five shelters," the task force coordinator said. "Colder weather has filled area shelters lately, and directors began turning away people weeks ago," she added.)

There but for, I write and stop, looking up, unable to shake the spooky sense that someone is watching me. After the others have gone to bed, the house announces itself: hum of neon, chug of refrigerator, clicking of timers. I hear my breathing, taken for granted like the other sounds and at one with them, hovering at the edge of consciousness, hidden by its comfortable familiarity, and noticeable only by its absence. Conspicuous like this it seems suddenly alien, the breathing of someone else. The gouged muffin face rises in the black window.

(Every night there are more . . . we don't turn them away . . . every night there are . . . we wash everything . . . every night there . . . we began turning them away weeks ago . . . every night . . . we're nervous . . . every night there are more. . . .)

The Unlived Life

In one unlived life, I wear black a lot, and my lover and I sometimes smudge our faces before going out at night. We eat food that comes in tins and drink a nameless Madeira from dark bottles, our plates and scraps left carelessly about the room. At night we listen to scratchy Lenny Bruce albums. Living with a stark, thoroughly committed, long-haired beauty from — oh — L.A. has its rewards. We read political tracts all day and make love on the floor when compelled by the passion of ideology or the ennui of philosophical texts. When she and the rest of the city go to sleep, I wire homemade bombs.

I don't worry about getting caught, though it will happen one day—unless I blow up the place after a careless slip or sneeze. What, after all, is one life? What I don't like is the sweet, almond taste of nitroglycerine—I can't get it off my fingers or out of the lace of her clothes, her one extravagance from a privileged past.

"Are you happy?" my beauty asks one night while we lie atop twisted sheets, smoking unfiltered cigarettes. Her voice is husky, without a trace of North Carolina in it, and though happiness is a bourgeois notion, I entertain the thought for a while, the smoke of our liberated lives puddling on the ceiling before it dissipates in the glow of one bare lightbulb.

I have, I admit, one nagging regret—a foolish notion, I tell her reluctantly. I'm tired of having all the answers. Killing, I say, demands certainty, and the certainty of it all gets to me. I would like to be able to ask a few real questions.

She looks away, and I see, by her glance, that she is only pretending to be disappointed.

In another unlived life I am poking my way down a long aisle of books, squinting at seemingly endless rows of Dewey decimals on cloth spines, a slip of paper in hand and a question on my lips. I like the dark—a dark aisle in an uninhabited corner of the library stacks. I also like to get lost, my question on urban terrorists changing as I wander by accident into the section on women's fashions. Arson and old lace, I think, chuckling to myself. If the room is dark and I get lost enough to forget my original question, so much the better. Then I know I'm on the right track.

The subject of my lifelong project is Josiah Royce and the American Idealists—not a particularly hot topic in our pragmatic times, a fact that pleases me. You would think I study the Torah, that's how reclusive my life has become. When people ask who my friends are I say Plato, Spinoza, and Ralph Waldo Emerson. I eat alone at night out of tins in the semidarkness of my bare kitchen, flipping through file cards in my mind, and whole days go by when I don't speak to a living soul.

I had a friend once—a sweet girl I met at Virginia Beach—and sometimes I hear her voice in my cluttered mind, just a hint of North Carolina in the accent. I was a dishwasher, and she first noticed me because I hid behind the cooler reading James Joyce. She could talk to a post, people said, and I, well, qualified, but I was too shy to do anything but hold her hand and walk silently along the beach. She is married with four kids, I hear. I keep cats, suffer the allergies, and take delight in setting six bowls of milk out each evening when I come home from the library.

Lately I worry because I laugh at my own jokes, and I wonder about myself when I pause in the gloomy aisle of floor nine, the question on the tip of my tongue dissolving my latest assurance. What would it be like to speak without thinking and act without hesitating, to stop wondering and start living? What would it be like to sleep with a woman?

Or, I shove the architect's table aside in frustration and stroll out the French doors of my beach bungalow to watch long, moonlit breakers line up neatly at the shoreline and crash on sand. All day I build castles, but only in the air. At night I come alive.

I'm alone for the time being, eating microwave dinners, so the beach looks even more beautiful to me. My last lover was a model for that designer—whatshisname?—the one who introduced combat boots and camouflaged vests to women's fashions. She was sleek, like water, and, like high tide among the rocks, insinuated herself into my comfortable days. With her around who could be bothered looking at the ocean?

After a few months we started to fight. She was spoiled. I was busy. I made spiteful asides and took long walks. I reminded her of a jellyfish, she said to a friend over the phone, an impossible combination of slimy and dull and dangerous, a remark I couldn't help overhearing—perhaps she intended that. One day she threw her camouflaged tops into a suitcase and left.

Now the ocean looks just fine.

Each year I seem to have a new lover, although for one period of about two years I didn't have one at all—and didn't miss it either. When I was young I nearly married that sweet girl from North Carolina (you know the one), but she fell for some writer and left—a lucky break for both of us, no doubt. Now I can have it all.

At the beach—there you feel free, every wave announcing in sibilant monotone that life is the accumulation of experiences, wave upon wave whispering "and . . . and . . . and . . . ," each as lovely as the last. I wouldn't want it any other way, believe me, because I am addicted to the flow of a new lover's hair across my bare arm, and yet there are nights, like tonight, when the waves whisper a different refrain. "*Not* this," they say, "nor this, nor this, but *this*," as a large, perfect tube of spun water roars to a consummation. If, for a time, I could believe anything wholeheartedly, I say at these moments of weakness, if there were some cause or some people for whom I would be willing to toss a bomb, maybe then my life would be worth living.

When life goes sour or falls short or turns dull, the imagination offers up an alternative, the unlived life, a daydream self. If the day hands me a power mower and a bag of groceries, my mind conjures up a lawnless life deep in the woods, far, far from any supermarket, where the trail leads to the base of cliffs overlooking the lapping sea and an adventure—please!—just over the horizon. "Oh, come *on*," my wife says when I get in these moods, a hint of North Carolina still in her voice. "You're driving me crazy." Angry, I walk out of the house, stamp to the car, and throw open the door only to find my other self, the anarchist, the scholar, the libertine, or some other other, glittering before my mind's eye, the choices I have made—wife, family, steady job—creating a shadow self, or more precisely shadowy selves, each arriving a bachelor to this family man.

"Have you looked in the mirror lately?" the ghosts hiss. "What don't you see there?"

Tales from German folklore offer a convenient explanation for these troublesome dream twins. A choice, according to these stories, creates a doppelgänger or double-goer, a duplicate self who lives out the life we do not choose. Ouch! Born of the fact that we have but one life and fed on unacted desire, the doppelgänger is our torment, and, according to tradition, meeting this simpering apparition is ominous. Death is always in the folds of his coat.

"Does the imagination dwell the most," William Butler Yeats wrote, "on the woman won or the woman lost?" Most of his life, Yeats was in love with Maud Gonne, the one he lost. He first met her in January 1889 when she stepped out of a hansom cab in front of his father's house. Tall and graceful, an actress with doleful eyes, high cheekbones, and precise lips shaped like petals about a weakness, she was in his opinion the most beautiful woman in the world, the soul of Ireland and a modern Helen of Troy. Her beauty, he wrote, was the kind that does not age.

Unfortunately, when they met, her life was already complicated by love. Attracted to men of action, she had given birth to a son in a secret love affair with a French political radical—a son who died several years later. Eventually, she married and had children by John MacBride, an alcoholic soldier who died a hero in the Easter Uprising of 1916.

What attracted Yeats to Maud Gonne, aside from her beauty, was her mystical nature. She once made love to a man in a burial vault in an attempt to reincarnate her dead son—a clue to this side of her. She often claimed that Yeats's soul visited hers in the middle of the night. Interested in anything mystical or visionary, Yeats was much taken by these eccentricities and even came to accept the fact that, with the exception of one carnal interruption in 1908, their love would remain excruciatingly spiritual. Who knows what that night was like? "Strike me if I shriek," Yeats wrote in a poem nineteen years later. A. Norman Jeffares, Yeats's biographer, suspects that these were Maud's words then — our solitary, tantalizing clue.

"Your poems are our children," she wrote to Yeats once, attempting to take the sting out of her many refusals to marry him, and all her life she claimed that she had done him and the world a favor by saying "no" to his proposals. There are hints, though, in the poetry, that Yeats often saw the missed opportunity for love as an evasion, at best a false sense of scruples and at worst an act of cowardice. In the poem "The Choice," he laments the empty virtues of a life dedicated to art rather than action, and in "The Tower" he writes of the torments of dwelling on the woman lost:

> . . . admit you turned aside
> From the great labyrinth out of pride,
> Cowardice, some silly over-subtle thought
> Or anything called conscience once.

Maud Gonne became for Yeats the "imagined image," a symbol of perfect beauty just out of reach that could not be coaxed into reality.

In ancient Greece, shippers tied down the statuary, fearing it would run away — it looked that real — and John Keats contemplated the urn, wondering if art might be an improvement on his short days on earth. Yeats read Plato and consoled himself, too, by creating poems about Maud Gonne, winning his love in song. But art does not replace life, and few of us are fooled forever. At night, his mind dwelling on missed opportunities, Yeats suffered "agony and tormented dreams." When the memory of lost love recurs, he wrote, the sun is "under eclipse and the day blotted out." No doubt he spent time in the deadly chambers of his doppelgänger.

Two A.M. My family all in bed. Suddenly a crack of thunder and a flash of light — the storm announces itself — and I am awakened by *my* doppelgänger, this time as a seventeen-year-old boy at the end of the bed. The lightning is nearly continuous, a phenomenon

I have not seen before, the room lit a shaky, iridescent white, robbing the world of color. Everything shimmers—the bureau, the quilt, my hand by Barbara's cheek as she sleeps—the flickerings converting skin to chalk and turning us into statues, shadowy, unearthly, and poetic.

It's dark in this reverie as the boy begins to enact an event of my life from nearly thirty years ago. I walk a young woman—a girl I would have said then—around the block in our small town in New Jersey. She wears a field hockey uniform, mud-smudged at the knees and thighs. Her hair, a little frizzy at the ends, has been pulled back in a convenient ponytail. She limps a bit, most likely a blister, and is very tired, but her face is scrubbed and she talks and talks, holding my hand happily. When we get to her door, a lit porch, we stop, and I know now I could kiss her and say, simply, "I love you," words that might have changed everything, but she has a boyfriend far away at college somewhere, so—out of goodness? temerity? cowardice?—I don't say a word, and, mumbling goodbye, walk back to my VW, hands shoved in pockets, a doppelgänger slipping out of the folds of my jacket as I shut the door.

How different it all would have been, I wonder now, remembering my young self circling the block several times and toying with going back, though I don't go back that night and never do, heading for college in North Carolina the next day myself, a different part of the country, meeting some other girl—because that's what we were then, boys and girls—and, walking with her along some dark beach, finding at last the courage to say those words and mean them and become a man. Of course, I wonder—who doesn't?—about that other life, different nights, different children.

I pass my open hand in front of my face and the apparition disappears. In the glare of the storm, the movement of my arm is cinematic, happening jerkily in front of my eyes like a sequence of still frames. Barbara's face looks unreal in this light—like someone's dream of Barbara, a mere image conjured up, it seems, by the mind. Her profile appears childlike in these shimmerings, lips pouted just a bit in sleep. It looks ancient, too, the bones at my fingertips apparent beneath a skin turned translucent. In the spectral glare, I touch her eyelash lightly, and the eyelid quivers without opening, alive and sensitive to touch.

"I have betrayed three people," Yeats thought a week into his marriage to Georgie Hyde-Lees. One of the people he thought he had betrayed was Maud Gonne's daughter. Despairing of ever marrying Maud, Yeats found himself in love with her winsome child, Iseult, and proposed, even though he was in his fifties and she barely out of her teens. When she turned him down, he asked Miss Hyde-Lees, who said yes. After a brief engagement Willie and George, as they called each other, were married, but no sooner had the honeymoon begun before Yeats fell into gloom, believing his marriage an act of cowardice and insanity: "I ran, I ran, from my love's side," he wrote, thinking of Iseult, "because my heart went mad."

The honeymoon, the marriage—and probably the great poet—were saved when George suddenly asked for paper while she and Yeats were dining one day. "I have lived all through this before," she said, announcing that something was to be written "through her." In a letter to a friend, Yeats described the scene: "She got a piece of paper, and talking to me all the while . . . wrote these words (which she did not understand), 'with the bird (Iseult) all is well at heart.'" To appease his doppelgänger, she added, wisely, a cryptic comment on his choices: "Your action was right for both in London you mistook its meaning."

So much for the bird.

This mystical moment sealed Yeats's love for George and began one of the most profitable literary and spiritual collaborations in history. He believed he had found a true soul mate, one who not only consoled him about his choices but also spoke in cryptic, evocative, images. For an hour or so each day he asked questions while his wife performed this automatic writing, offering her husband "metaphors for poetry."

Love, he happily discovered, is not a pose or an image, but a relationship, a dialogue of the soul and a translation of the spirit. There is, he also came to see, an inevitable falling off at consummation. "Maybe the bride bed brings despair," he wrote in "Solomon and the Witch," "for each an imagined image brings and finds a real image there." But love, he recognized, required the maturity to discard such images in order to achieve a richer sense of self. The perfected image of love is not what counts, except as we find it transformed in a beloved's eye.

A real image. Soon the storm begins to subside, the lightning becoming intermittent again, and I watch for a long time, amazed by a simple fact: between each heave of light, I find myself eager for the next flash, so that I can have another look. Taken away, the image of my wife's face acquires the nostalgia of all lost things, but each time the room lights up, the face takes shape again—the real image, the parenthesis in the syntax of my daydreams, the Carolina accent in my days, and the doppelgänger of all my unlived lives.

I remember the girl in the hockey shorts. The last time I saw her, years ago, we didn't talk. She was available by then, I heard, but I was deeply in love. In love and a different person, I realize now, recognizing that the unlived life is not a specter life, some idealized other, because none of the people involved exist. They are arrested in a past they refused to nudge into the future. The boy who might have lived up to a moment years ago simply was not ready to become anyone other than the man writing this page whose joys and woes, such as they are, have taken their unique turn.

Some require a blow, Dostoyevsky wrote. One required automatic writing. For me a storm helped. The intervals between the flashes of light grew longer and were followed, inevitably, by the crack and rumble of the night and my own desire to look again. In the dark I weigh the losses: a bomb thrower, a bookworm, a playboy, a shriek in the night—all images illuminated by impossibility. Robed in death, they don't weigh much. All that I have is here and alive. In this light and under my constant scrutiny it becomes real, again and again and again.

I woke up feeling so sad this morning because I realized
that you could not, as much as I love you,
dear heart, cure my loneliness.

ROBERT HASS

The Ordinary Hours

I picture the lovers sipping coffee alfresco by the sea the day after a night of wide-eyed lovemaking, my imagination altering the poem I have just read. She announces that nothing, not even this love, can cure her loneliness, and the man, her dear heart, reluctantly agrees, the lovers becoming by the last line "merely companionable." Since the poem stops here, I set the book face-down on the porch swing and imagine that the orange umbrella in the wrought-iron table between them suddenly lifts in a breeze, blows in an ungainly tumble across the beach, and flops like a wounded gull, into the ocean where it sags, soaking in brine. The lovers stand, she holding her wide-brimmed hat in place as it slaps about her eyes, and he shoving both hands deep in his pockets.

If passion does not keep our umbrellas aloft, what, then, do lovers have left to share? Sex cheats death, the poet says elsewhere, but only for an hour or so. Then what? After cartwheeling into the seas of another, does the spent lover merely drift through the other hours even more lonely, the spokes and pastels of momentary joys dragged under by the monotonous rhythms of the surf? What can be said about the plain stepsister of passion, the rest of our lives? I hear my wife in the house vacuuming and singing, hundreds of miles from coffee alfresco by any sea. What about the ordinary hours, I think, when we become ourselves?

On bright afternoons among glittering kitchen knives, Barbara and I bump into each other enough to know that in our loneliness we are rarely alone. I break open the lettuce head with both hands while she reaches past me for a dish. She is talking to one of the kids, and I feel her other hand on my shoulder—for balance, for love—as she rises on tip-toe. I'm here, this touch says—a message and a reminder—like the hand of a basketball player on the shirt of an opponent.

Later, when I'm dicing mushrooms, the conversation heats up. We begin to argue about the role of sports in the lives of children, and I turn quickly, pointing the knife blade for emphasis. Startled, we look at the gleaming thing between us. "Don't worry," she says turning the blade away with one finger, "French dressing will hide the blood!" We laugh, and I go back to fixing lunch, laying my open hand above the knife and cutting through the sandwich, my body rising a bit as the blade sinks into the food we share.

Sometimes a glance is all we can afford. It can happen anywhere. Barbara tries on our daughter's prom dress, the family applauding in the den, and just before her mouth turns up ironically, she looks at me—eyes widening slightly—and whatever happens wordlessly between us lasts the entire length of the kids' not noticing before she turns to our blushing nine-year-old boy, who wears his ball cap backward on his head. "Shall we dance?" she says, with a curtsy. When he runs off, she winks at me.

These gestures—a wink, a pat, or a hug—can rescue our dun days. Once or twice a week Barbara and I cross each other on the highway—going on separate errands, with different kids in each car—and before I can say "look, there's your mom," she's past us, her wave a feeble flicker on the windshield, lovely in its banality, another of those incongruous situations that love asks us to bear. Stolen from the grid of our scheduled lives, such gestures redeem our toil.

Much loving is, in fact, toil, love and sweat never separated for long. On the days that we weed the garden, I take the clattering cart into the woods and gather the mulch. I pull the loam to my chest, holding it there against my shirt. Soon my shirt and the woods' floor are about the same color. Barbara weeds and points—"We need some—uh—here," she says—inevitably smudging her cheek and forehead as she wipes away sweat.

She smiles when she works, aware always of what's to be done and glad to be doing it, her eyes moving faster than her hands. I groan a lot. I clear a spot around the geraniums only to find that I have, in the process, trampled the ageratum. When we are done for the day, we stand side by side and look at our work—the flower bed stripped of grass and clover, the lilies and bee balm standing erect, the ageratum, a mangle of stems but green nonetheless, all tucked in with a thick layer of black leaves and loamy earth, the dead offerings of our woods. We don't say much. We don't need to.

There are times at night when Barbara and I talk on the porch, the dark world around us lit by one light, our voices like hands gentling something down—the dog of death, perhaps, that has pawed its way into our conversation and lowered a muzzle in the space between us on the swing. It is not what we say but the sounds against the silences beyond us—the tones of frankness and mutual confusion—that soothe the beast. The pause between "well" and "I don't know, either," a hideaway where the shadow of her words closes on the shadow of mine.

Some nights, in summer, a breeze shares us—becomes the animating spirit of all that remains unsaid in the commonplaces we pass back and forth. Like a limb falling among branches, like meets like in these conversations, breaking the fall to the woods' floor. So our talk, fits of language and long pauses, slows our dark descent, though words crack and fail us. If we are lucky, we are released from the demons of ourselves. Mind drifts past this lit place, is lost, we say, in thought, and finds a soft bed of leaves in the moonlight clearing of no thoughts at all, resting there, far off, and we are alone together in the oblivion we all must eventually learn.

Later, before falling asleep, we speak a few words, and the sounds, nocturnal versions of our daily chatter, scamper off to dark corners and hang lemur-like in shadows, gazing back at us, their eyes filled with arboreal wonder. Barbara likes to rest her head on my shoulder briefly—it's my job to provide a shoulder, she says—and I rub her hair, a happy mammalian gesture. Then we tug the covers to our chins and turn to our separate nights.

Ultimately, we sleep alone, our lover's body and our body left behind when the muscles jerk spasmodically, releasing us to our somnolent selves. I am a dreamer. Not long after we got married I sat upright in bed in the middle of the night and saw in a triangle of light above the bureau the image of Buster Brown and his dog on the wall. "Look!" I said to my new bride, who raised herself dutifully on one elbow and squinted at the patch of reflected light. In other dreams, burglars have stolen into the house, my children have fallen out of my grasp down a well, or, worse, arms aching, I have been forced to choose one child and watch the other fall—always waking in a sweat before I make the choice. Men with hatchets have stalked menacingly behind curtains in my nightmares, and a thug with a stocking mask has pointed the barrel of his rifle at the door and looked at my wife.

Other dreams are more benign, though they all suggest responsibility. I have leapt out of bed and thrown on clothes, getting as far as the front door before realizing that it was the middle of the night, and I hadn't missed the classes I teach. Once I dreamed that my son's entire graduating class had lined up with candles and robes by the road in front of my house, and I was on the porch about to say a few words to the crowd before the candles turned to fireflies and the long gowns of Matt's friends hardened into the familiar trunks of poplar, oak, and pine lined up across the street.

Barbara no longer wakes up with me, as she did that first night, saying sweetly, after she touched the lit place on the wall, "I don't see Buster Brown *or* his dog, Steve." I'm lucky now to get a groan, but it is always a comfort when the darkness sheds the shapes of my torments and becomes just darkness again to feel the weight of someone beside me. All that we share is real, these groggy moments teach me. The rest is but a dream.

Most mornings I wake up first. Barbara sleeps with one leg poking out from the swirled sheets and blanket, the rest of her tucked away in bedding, all but the hair that—rumpled from the night—falls in a tumble over the pillow. Most of the time she lies still, arms and legs at angles, like someone dropped from a great height, a silly, almost pathetic, sprawl. Occasionally she moves, pulling absently at the covers below her shoulder with her fingers or shifting her whole body weight under the blankets, rearranging the warmths there before settling into the deeper stillness of a body intent on oblivion. When I leave the bed, she stretches out so that she has my side and hers, too, and takes my pillow, breathing into it—her breath the only sound in the room. Watching nearby, I know that even if I were in bed with her, my lap her pillow and she with her arms around my waist, I would not be closer or less alone.

So which is it? Closer? Or less alone? Or—as the poet put it—a little of both, our ordinary woes rendering lovers "merely companionable?"

Barbara and I are great walkers, and I think we take walks, oddly enough, in order to shed the rigors of love and become, for an hour or so, merely companionable — to be with each other what we are with the world. A turn down Maple Street brings us to friends sitting out on stoops or leaning against cars, and with them we are our other selves. We shake hands, brush sleeves, and pet dogs. Our words, I notice, relax into sentences, no longer the telegrammatic, gnomic utterances of the bedroom or porch, no longer just a glance or mood clue, but the syntax of conversation in which we claim positions, state resolutions, tell jokes, and make plans. With love on hold, we become acquaintances again, and all that we say is what we bargained for or less.

At the beach, Barbara wears dark glasses and tanning lotion, and her body, draped over a blanket, is given up to the sun in plates of light that crash among the blues and beiges of the ocean. Her name, in fact, means stranger and at the beach she claims her title. By day the skin at her arms and neck and shoulders turns pink — a borrowed glow — and at night when the slip falls away from her shoulders, the pink has deepened to brown, a cinnamon hue, and gives off a faint smell of anise. I cannot — on these days stolen from our real selves — resist touching the tan line, the boundary of our world, where the self I know ends and the stranger, the *barbara* she has become, begins.

Estrangement is usually not benign, though, and on nights that I cannot sleep, it turns sinister. In the shadows of three A.M. Barbara can be infuriatingly far away, her face, involuntarily but inevitably, taking on the smug expression of a sleeper. She doesn't need to appear so at ease while I pace the floor, I grumble, or so beatific while I sit glumly in a circle of yellow light turning pages. We are not in separate worlds then as we are when we sleep. She is in hers and I am in ours, and by four o'clock the whole thing seems so unfair that a mighty effort is required on my part not to touch her shoulder and say "hey," but I don't — the demons of an insomniac are not to be shared — and wait instead for the bedroom windows to turn pink again and for her to roll over, reach past my pillow, and say my name as a question, signaling the end of my ordeal.

Sometimes our moods take a toll, falling into a binary pattern that turns us into antagonists. Like the Dutch boy and girl on the clock, an inexplicable gloominess on my part brings Barbara out, wearing a false smile in consolation, but no sooner does the gloom in me pass, the little door opening on my newly acquired smile, than she retreats, her face transformed into a frown as the manikin of her happy mood disappears, with a click and a cuckoo, behind a small door. I find myself snapping and buzzing and clicking center-stage, then, Chaplinesque and all alone, my lacquered smile in place. Old betrayals come back, and words spoken in anger months, maybe years, ago, words that have been waiting for us to turn into mechanical dolls on separate tracks, words that send us hurtling down the highway of our certain deaths in separate cars with no more than the flicker of a wave on the windshield to console us.

Occasionally, estranged by grief, we are driven past all smiles into parts of ourselves far from each other and wear faces no husband or wife recognizes. When Barbara's father died she called me at the office. "Come home," she said in a girl's voice and started to cry. I dropped everything and drove to her, though there was nothing that I could do — nothing that my presence could undo either. No pat, no hug, no glance of mine would bring him back, but I rushed home anyway to touch and hold her and look in her eyes. She drove to her mother's that night alone, and I worried about her, fatherless for the first time, heading down a dark highway and arriving — drained — to a grieving house and an empty room. Death eventually brings us to an empty room. "Not a day has gone by," she told me a year later, "when I have not thought of him," and even now when she reads this, she will cry at the memory and be alone.

I know that the woman in the poem is right about lonely places in us that no lover can reach. I find them in myself, days when my umbrella sags and the monotony of my nights opens a deep pit.

Others, we learn sooner or later, cannot help us then, no matter how much we love them or they requite our love. We return from such interior excursions, if return is possible, wearing sunglasses and handing out souvenirs, knowing that loneliness has no cure.

But even though our condition is incurable, there is, for the lifetime of the victim, the possibility of containment. When I sing to the children at night Barbara sometimes joins in, harmonies hovering like invitations around any lone melody line, each note implying another voice. She sits in Sam's bed, playing with his hair, and when Alice wiggles into range she holds her too, rubbing her leg. They get calm under her hands, these restless scoundrels that we made while cheating death on lonesome evenings. She and I find our singing parts tentatively, listening to each other and watching, cocking eyebrows hopelessly when we hit a sour note but smiling when we get it right. The children smile, too, and eventually fall asleep. In the midst of this fully domesticated moment, we make what beauty we can, the single note never usurped but surrounded by harmony.

Intimacy is best expressed in such moments—a song, a joke, and a glance—the synecdoches of love. Lovers don't keep death and loss away, and in the end we let go of each other's hand as we close our eyes on our agonies. But for now we have someone to talk to at night, companionable but not merely so, and during our days we shake a picnic blanket between us, opening it to the wind as it floats at last to a grassy spot among the books and bottles of our daily lives.

America

So many hauses: Wursthaus, Strudel Haus, Tobak Haus, Gessellschaft Haus, Riverhaus Pizza, and—best of all—Haus of Glitter and Fantasy. Is this Germany? Austria? Hardly. It is Helen, Georgia, a faux Alpine Village at the southern tip of Appalachia about an hour south of where I live, a bit of Americana gone berserk. Linguistic bastardizations hang above almost every shoppe door here: Das Ist Leather, Horsie and Ducky Platz, Harmoniemusik, Edelweiss Deli, and—ugh!—a perfume shop named Let's Make Scents.

Such names!—and they are just the beginning. Inside the Haus of Glitter and Fantasy, one of the hundreds of stores in Fantasy Alley, which runs through this Alpine purgatory, are ashtrays and glasses and gems of all kinds with the name and image of Helen embossed on them. A table is filled with mugs that have a heart on them and the phrase "Helen is for lovers"—all lined up neatly with most of the phrase hidden to create a seemingly endless, amorous string of "overs." And in the Indian section, the faces of Rambo and Indiana Jones are painted on wooden machetes beside drawings of chiefs on stretched leather.

Down the platz, at the Old Helendorf Inn, a cement lion gapes at the door. New street lamps made to look old with twin-spired ironwork fixtures are like something out of Dickens, and flags from far away and long ago hang limp on a lintel above a sidewalk covered with torn indoor-outdoor carpet of a green color that has never appeared in nature. The windows have a Renaissance look, diamond-shaped panes and wooden shutters, and the window boxes are graced with Christmas greenery year-round. Only barn swallows, flitting under false stucco arches, look indigenous.

Townies sit under freshly made old-world awnings, picking neighbors out from the tourists and waving. All day they answer the same questions: yes, the coffee's good, they say, parking is a problem, they admit, and pointing up the strasse, explain that the bathroom is over there. Tourists capture it all on videocams slung over their shoulders, recording forever all the quaint atmosphere that wasn't here twenty-five years ago. Like tourists everywhere, they are slim and fat, giddy and bored, and dressed in neon colors no one would be caught dead in at home.

Most of them are couples. A man in an orange windbreaker strolls hand-in-hand with a woman in green jeans and silk blouse, her long ponytail dangling from the opening at the back of her baseball cap. Behind them a pregnant woman in a hot-pink blouse and black pants conscientiously ignores her enormous husband, who is draped in a Braves T-shirt with a red and blue tomahawk splashed across the front. Not far from them a woman in hot pants and halter top and sandals—all openings—tugs at the sleeve of her man, who sports deck shoes, a purple shirt, a beard, and a toupee. Looking at these couples I am reminded that Helen (as the cups say) *is* for lovers, lovers cut free from reality and promenading in pairs through the cerements of a Bavaria from nowhere.

A plaque in front of the Bavarian Haus says it all: "On This Site in 1987 Nothing Happened." Exactly. How on earth would you ever know *what* happened in this town built out of everywhere else? And yet, amid the glitter, there are hints of a real history. The Wildewood Shoppe, on a back street, makes little more than a gesture toward the European with its pastel window jambs and the phoney "e's" in the name. The rest of the building slumps authentically in the mountain tradition and is a pure product of the Georgia hills: rusted tin roof, slatted porch, an unpainted, flimsy, two-by-four porch rail, and a sprawl of additions, done one room at a time, each with a newer, shinier, metal roof.

Rhododendron and mountain laurel still line the bank along the river as they have for centuries. I take a path that leads under the bridge and even though I am at the heart of town—delivery trucks rumbling overhead—I get a glimpse of what this spot used to be. Seeing cement foundation stones tumbled along the bank side, I think of the old lumber mills from a century ago. Watching the river glitter here and there before it turns into the dark thickets, I think of Indian settlements, too, and remember the ancient source of all that is here, the Indian mound at the southern edge of town—a primordial site for glittering ceremonies.

Eventually, though, my eyes drift back to street level, pretty waitresses taking orders under *Cinzano* umbrellas and an Austrian flag flapping in the breeze, and the actual past is shattered. I am suddenly returned to the obviously repellent but oddly comfortable stucco and false-beam architecture of the town of Glitter and

Fantasy. Looking at it — taking it all in — creates a distinctly American sense of living nowhere and the accompanying feeling of being nowhere alive.

Helen was not always this way. According to the *History of Helen* by Carole Proctor Scruggs, the dream village was invented one day in the spring of 1968 while Jim Wilkins, Bob Fowler, and Pete Hodkinson were eating lunch at the steak house. Looking out the plate-glass window at the dilapidated storefronts of their bust lumber town, Pete said, "you know, Helen could really be a pretty place." Who knows what his mind's eye saw that day as he looked across the river at the depressing Main Street. It hardly matters. What he got was Helen — so did we.

First, the town leaders hired the artist John Kolloch, who arrived in the area at sunset and, fatefully, decided to pull his car off the road at a scenic spot overlooking the town. By an act of will his imagination eradicated reality from the scene — "the buildings of the town were almost invisible," he said later, and added, "the fog had a dreamlike quality that helped my woolgathering." At that moment he had his vision: "I felt suddenly as if I were back in one of the villages in Bavaria where I had spent a year in the services." Before he had set foot in the town, Kolloch had had his vision; before he had unpacked, Helen was reborn as a dream.

The timetable for constructing the dream was nightmarish. Kolloch photographed buildings and, after reviewing snapshots and postcards from Bavaria, drew up facades for each one. These drawings were taken to George Washington Westmoreland, the owner of a garage in the center of a row of stores. "I'm ready when you are!" he said. Called the "Chief" by locals, his participation was crucial — soon the other owners fell in line. "I don't know the difference between a Swiss chalet and a geisha house," contractor Roy Sims admitted when asked to head up the construction — a revealing confusion. He, too, was game: "we'll do it," he said.

Ten months later it was done.

Never did the planners lose sight of the goal, the replacement of reality with a photogenic dream: a town made pretty in the eye of the beholder. Quality control was a high priority. "As we worked," Kolloch said, "I kept photographing the buildings to check and see that each would make an easy composition for the tourist camera." The new facades of buildings were painted, depicting scenes of what had been lost, effigies to the nature that the village had usurped. The most famous of these is a painting of Anna Ruby Falls on the stucco front of a shop, the painted falls tumbling from either side of a roofbeam to the street below, the sidewalk stippled with blood-red droplets. It makes a pretty picture, I thought, putting my finger to the painted stone. Gingerbread awnings, silent bell towers, steep-pitched rooftops—amid all this Gretel, little of the old mountain girl, Helen, remains.

The name Helen comes from the lumbering days of the town, though it seems no more authentic than the Bavarian transplant. John Mitchell, a real estate promoter, shrewdly named the land south of Robertstown after the daughter of the railroad executive who supplied his buyers. There is no evidence that little Helen ever set foot in the place.

What remains of the old lumbertown that was Helen can be found along the river. A high-water marker rises fifteen feet out of the river suggesting the size of flood crests created by splash dams in the logging days several generations ago. Weathered stones, obviously old enough to go back to the time of the Byrd Matthews Lumber Company, line the banks, and in the background a saw whines through two-by-fours at a construction site, a sound reminiscent of the groaning blade that planed trees six-feet thick and bigger more than eighty years ago. In the garden behind the hotel, a large, weathered concrete block holds a place—a hulking presence. Like crossed arms, it says power and looks forever on water, a sullen souvenir.

The mill and railroad were in place by 1912, and in 1913 the boom began, a time of wealth and waste. Splash dams, used to create sudden floods, allowed logs to be carried downriver, but often the rush of water split timber or ran it aground at shallows, where it rotted, and logs tumbled over the edge of waterfalls at an enormous loss. One logger who worked the Matthews operation estimated that more than a million feet of timber was lost at Anna Ruby Falls alone. Most of the logs made their way downstream, nonetheless, and at Nora Mills, south of town, as much as 125,000 board feet of lumber could be cut daily, enormous pine and poplar boards twenty feet long and four feet wide, to be shipped to Gainesville and Atlanta.

At fifty cents a board foot on the stump, prosperity came to Helen, taking the form of a drugstore, a bank, and Maloof's General Merchandise Store. In 1913 Burt Matthews opened a commissary, which according to one local had a "fabulous" inventory of "silk, thread, ribbons, clothing, groceries, overalls, shirts, and meat." The town had three telephones and, by 1914, a weekly newspaper, the *Helen Herald*. In the summer, locals walked to baseball games fifteen miles away for amusement, and in the winter these enterprising souls hauled ice over slushy trails by mules shod with cork.

Quick riches were nothing new to the mountain people of Helen, though. Earlier, in the 1820s, gold had been discovered there and mined for more than thirty years. The find, occurring a few years before the more famous one at Dahlonega, was the beginning of America's first great gold rush. Before it was done, Helen produced more than two million pennyweight of gold worth more than a million dollars, and the county's population nearly doubled.

Gold, lumber, tourists—Helen has always made money. In this, it has followed—in fact, exceeded—the pattern for towns and villages in the area. John Parris, a local historian, best described the pattern: "All we want here is to get the most out of this country as quickly as we can, and then get out." By 1861 the gold was gone. By

1925 the virgin timber of America's southeastern old wood forests was gone, too. One minister in the region at the time lamented the losses. "While this work, of course, has given employment to the natives of the mountains," the Reverend A. E. Brown said to the Southern Baptist Convention in 1910, "it is destroying the future for them." His words were prophetic.

Eventually mills in Helen were gone, the saws dismantled and sent west to new tree sites in Mexico, and the boomtown went bust. Dilapidated and abandoned buildings marked the grave, the same buildings that Pete Hodkinson saw when he looked out the steak house window in 1968. But when he spoke about Helen's wrecked future, the Reverend Brown didn't mention that sudden prosperity had destroyed another future as well; the discovery of gold in the mountains in 1828 had led, almost immediately, to the removal of those who had a prior claim to the land: the Cherokees.

The last Cherokee to live in the Nacoochee valley near Helen was Sam Wingo, who made butter paddles for the dairy, wove baskets, and caned chair bottoms. Who knows how he escaped the Trail of Tears. This valley, just south of Nora Mills, with a glorious Indian mound at the western end, was one of the gathering points for Indians rounded up by Winfield Scott—Old Fuss and Feathers—for the forced march out of Georgia in 1838. Perhaps Wingo escaped and, as his name suggests, hid in caves at higher elevations, like other Indians. Perhaps he was simply overlooked in the confusion.

According to Gloria Jahoda's book, *The Trail of Tears*, spring was particularly beautiful that year: "azaleas burned in the hollows; the pale pink blooms of mountain laurel bobbed gently in winds." She paints an Edenic picture with ominous hints that the idyll was temporary. "Cherokee children ran laughing in the squares," and—amid rumors of forced removal—natives told one white farmer that they would "prefer death to Arkansas." No doubt Jahoda is right when she says that "Winfield Scott's soldiers were an unreal dream."

Soon enough the dream turned into a nightmare. Scott's officers were instructed to seize the Indians at dinnertime, when they were least likely to suspect, but the soldiers took them any time and anywhere they found them—women were dragged from kitchens, children abducted at play in yards, men taken in fields where they worked. Families were divided—mothers given no time to gather up children—and all were herded with the animals into pens.

"The Cherokees are nearly all prisoners," Evan Jones reported in the *Baptist Missionary Magazine*. He described families shoved out of their houses, women cursed by troops and driven on foot at gunpoint, and property sold for "almost nothing" on the spot.

> The poor captive, in a state of distressing agitation, his weeping wife almost frantic with terror, surrounded by a group of crying, terrified children, without a friend to speak a consoling word, is in a poor condition to make a good disposition of his property, and in most cases is stripped of the whole, at one blow.

"This is not a description of extreme cases," Jones went on to say. "It is altogether a faint representation of the work which has been perpetrated on the unoffending, unarmed, and unresisting Cherokees."

Some Indians did fight back. Jahoda recounts one story of an Indian named Tsali, who came to the defense of his wife. Like others, she had been poked with a bayonet. When Tsali saw the insult, he showed no emotion but that night slit the soldier's throat. After months of eluding authorities in mountain caves, he and his family turned themselves in under the agreement that none of the other Indians hiding in caves would be harmed. Led before the firing squad, Tsali and his sons stood stoically, refusing blindfolds.

The removal of the Cherokees to the southwest corner of the Arkansas territory—modern Oklahoma—lasted through the winter. The Indians call this "The Trail Where We Cried." According to Jahoda, "a quarter of the Cherokee Nation died." After the

Cherokees left Georgia, the whites burned their houses and took the land. There is little sign of that brutality here now, the Nacoochee valley green to the river in early spring. Visitors can find arrowheads in the field and read roadside markers that claim that De Soto, searching for gold in 1540, stopped at this spot, a Cherokee town named Quaxule. The ugliness of beatings and forced exile is gone, lost amid the beauty of this valley and the glitz of nearby Helen. Only the mound, in a fenced off pasture south of town, has the solemnity to suggest what happened here.

Even the Cherokees who lived in its shadow did not know who built the mound, nor did they understand its original purpose. It was lost to them — a relic — like the lumbertown to today's tourists at Helen. In 1915 the Heye Foundation, sponsored by the Smithsonian Institution, conducted an excavation and found the answer. They discovered that an earthen stairway once led to the mound's flattened top. There, inside a circular town house at the summit, a continuous fire burned and ceremonial dances were held. Excavating lower, the Smithsonian team found seventy-five graves.

The settlement at the mound near Helen was probably a satellite community of the Southern Death Cult, a native civilization that flourished along the rivers in Tennessee and Georgia around A.D. 700. The town was a commercial center with an elaborate political hierarchy, including a priestly class that performed spectacular rituals. According to evidence from the digs, the priests, at the death of a town leader, would transform the plaza into the site of an all-consuming ceremony for the dead.

If these rites were like the ones in nearby Etowah, Eagle-being dancers decked in bead and conch shell pendants and wearing a copper plate headdress and hair ornament would lift their feet high in the air as they waved a copper baton and shook a wooden rattle carved in the shape of a head. Lit by torches, these dancers were no doubt striking and mysterious as they sang chants in a rich and glittering garb, warding off anxieties about death with their frightening gestures. The dead were buried with ornately carved artifacts representing all their worldly goods, circles and crosses embossed in silver and copper or carved into stone or shell gorgets, symbols of the abundance and wealth that cannot be carried beyond the grave. In some Death Cult mounds the eyes of the dead were covered with stones or shells or hidden behind elaborately beaded forelocks — the last resort of a people afraid to die.

The power of the mound is at least sexual, the arched back of earth rising in desire here to as much of the sky as the mountains ever have to offer, announcing itself when I come into its presence as the center of all, the long grassy meadow strewn about it in the droopy shapes of detumescence. It conjures up images of gestation and nurture, a grassy place reminiscent of the breast and surrounded by cattle. Standing at its flattened top I take in, at a glance, acres of land that have fed people and livestock for more than a thousand years. The mound, built to ease death fear, surveys prosperity and wealth — all that the living have to lose.

Spring happens easily here, I see — the creek off to the south lined with budded laurel and rhododendron that hide the shaggy shanks of cottonwoods. The meadow itself is dotted with daisies and hung here and there with white patches of Queen Anne's lace. The mound — eroded, smoothed by ages and mown — hunches, a light green shoulder of April grasses dotted with daisies. It is a place set aside, holy, the site once of a temple, and even though it sits exposed to traffic, cows, and a stream of curious tourists like me, it remains apart from what it surveys.

The mound suggests all of this — desire, nurture, holiness — but it is in fact a grave, and like all grave markers (the facades of Helen, the stones of the lumber town, the arrowheads in the corn fields) it measures our loss and fits us for reality. Loss is the first impulse I feel in its presence, the sense that this is a remnant, a clue, to mysteries that escape us still — to losses that our wealth cannot protect us from. The gingerbread gazebo, built on top of the mound by a former governor, and a hint of the present Helen at its ancient source, is no doubt a gesture to compensate for that sense of loss, the intricate wood railings and ornamental red tin roof an attempt by a later time to fill a void. In its tracery I see that the hauses and strasses and platzes of Helen are only the latest of countless removals, the newest monument to our ancient, death-driven greed.

Barn swallows nest in the gazebo and fly into the evening meadow in a wild, tumbling search for insects. They look from here like shaman hands fluttering from invisible sleeves. The mound, our source and culmination, casts an oblong shadow into the open field, darkening the grasses. Here the dead were buried with shells over their eyes and the past forsaken, then as now, for a continuous and increasingly gaudy present of dreams and glitter. A truck in low gear roars by. Loaded with goods, it is all that remains of the ancient, torch-lit Eagle dancers, the headlights casting eerie beams into the trees as it heads into America, toward Atlanta and beyond, away from the dead that it never really leaves behind.

The Changed Name of God

Suddenly snow, a blanching of air, the nearly weightless bodies, "manna" the poet John Logan calls them, falling "as wedding rice," blown high in crosswinds or riding dreary, dreamy paths to the ice-rutted, brown-thatched, mudslicked ground, changing the gray scene, the woolen sky, folded mountains, and endless, herringbone thickets of leafless hardwoods to the white of swirled sheets, and plunging the world into brightness.

Before the snow, I had crunched down the gravel path from my house in a sour mood, hoping to tramp away sullenness. I stamped past the fallen, lop-limbed, vine-twirled shaft of a hickory at the roadside, past the ancient graveyard with makeshift, weathered, upright river-stone markers, past the creek carrying its glitter forever somewhere else. Determined and undirected, I trudged beyond my neighbor's upturned wheelbarrow, the handles pointed with abstract and unfocused deliberateness at nothing overhead. Along slopes, brittle grasses twisted wildly but failed to hide the reddish-brown scalp of mud underneath or the beer cans, tinsel, and napkins sucked into the ooze. Crossing a culvert, I left behind, or tried to leave behind, news reports of chemical warfare and laser-guided weapons ripping into exhausted and wretched bodies. I trudged on, head down.

"Here endless walks circle about around bottomless dams," the Swedish poet Gunnar Ekelöf wrote, describing the deadness of spirit that we do not walk away from. "Here the days all reflect one monotonous day." I tramped through the grass to a dry hump of land at the lake's margin where I stopped and looked long at the uniformly dimpled surface, the windblown waves, the agitated water shirring at my feet.

Less, the water said gathering into waves, *less*, and *less*.

Then, suddenly, snow.

The wind lifted the "small, terrible bodies," and the flakes, losing their desultory ways, slashed on the horizontal and gashed the sky whiter with each gust, going with the land now and against the trees and flung the length of open fields and roads in a dizzying, silver buckshot rush, riding strong currents—mounting and scattering in the counterwinds—but settling at last among gray-shafted oaks, leafy branches, and shaggy, green-skirted pines, covering surely, silently, the mud along the roads and the thick mulch of the woods' floor.

Yes—suddenly snow.

"Snow," John Logan wrote in "Spring of the Thief," will "fill these fields" and "change this hill." It will "transform" all. Feeling melancholy after a Lenten service, the speaker in the poem—Logan himself, no doubt—comes upon statues of Christ and the thieves at crucifixion, and even though the "ice is gone from the lake" and the air "altered" from what it was, he is struck by his memory of the same statues in winter when they were half-hidden in a whirl of snow, the flakes "blooming in the light." Looking at the statues Logan feels guilty, like a thief himself.

He describes a bizarre and humiliating night the winter before in which he reveled naked beneath "the howling January moon," and digging his "fist" into "the cold winter sand," hid his "manhood" under snow. Someone had to take him home that night, and later he felt shame, wondering who had dressed him:

> Washed up at some ancient or half heroic shore
> I was ashamed that I was naked there
> Before Nausicäa and the saints. Before myself.
> But who took off my coat? Who put it on?
> Who drove me home?

Now, looking at the spring statues but remembering winter, he wants to "confess" or "simply talk," but the doors of the "Mammoth Sacred Heart Church" are locked. What is God's "winter name," he asks, as Gunnar Ekelöf had asked before him. "Where is his winter home?"

In the late thirties Ekelöf lived in isolation in "the Yellow Cottage" in Hölo, Sweden, a small town south of Stockholm. It was a "trying time," he wrote in a memoir, the beginning of World War II and of Finland's Winter War with the Soviets, which broke out in November 1939 after Nordic leaders—meeting only a few miles away—refused to come to the aid of the Finns. In the battle, the Finns were "superb, nay sublime," Winston Churchill said, their troops on skis outflanking and outmaneuvering an enormous Soviet army that was not supplied well or dressed for the frigid climate, but by February the tide had turned and the Soviets fought their way across the Finnish frontier and captured Vyborg. Finnish blood joined Russian blood in the snow. Within a year, the Nazis answered the Soviet victory in Finland by invading and occupying Denmark and Norway. Sweden alone was free.

What do you do if you are a pacifist in Sweden during the Hitler years? What indeed. You reject your enemies and reject your allies and reject and reject and reject. You go deep into yourself in the hope of finding relief from the great human contradiction—the turning of the bloodied cheek, the glazed look of the doll falling from a hand, the insanity of tanks. You flee the cities and find a landscape as remote and barren as your inner life, doing so in the cold, wild hope of building on emptiness. You visit hospitals when it snows and listen to the mad, waiting for the heavy, white-bodied snow birds to return.

When the war began, Ekelöf decided that God, like the petal, the swan, and the snowflake, does not—in the face and fist of evil—take sides. He, too, felt like a thief, an outlaw beyond morality at a time when good and evil divided the world, and had come to believe that "the impractical is the only thing practical in the long run." He retreated to the remote town of Dorotea and tried to become a "useless person."

Poets are thieves. Logan draws on Ekelöf to write his finest poem; Ekelöf himself spent a good deal of time answering Swedish critics who accused him of relying too heavily on T. S. Eliot. "My poems do not express, do not contain the same thing as his," he complained. Despite his disavowals, Ekelöf was enamored of Eliot, had "long passages by heart," could produce translations from memory of the originals, and published Swedish versions of Eliot's "East Coker." As for Eliot, "poets do not borrow," he wrote, "they steal"—turning the poet's lonely quarrel with the world into a lovers' spat.

In the midst of World War II—with Sweden surrounded by occupied countries—T. S. Eliot defied the German blockade of England and flew to Stockholm for a presentation. Ekelöf traveled across the Swedish countryside during the long polar night to see him. Unfortunately, plans were botched, and all that could be arranged was a hurried encounter at the train station. "The same day that Eliot arrived," Ekelöf wrote, "I took the night train back to Lapland and wasn't able to meet him." In the margin of this note his wife added, "except five minutes." Having squandered the moment on little more than a handshake with Eliot, Ekelöf headed back by train gazing out over the backlit terrain of his beleaguered homeland, the land of the midnight sun.

Among the papers he returned to was the poem "The Swan." In it life is reduced to a hospital grounds of endless walkways leading nowhere. Flowers withdraw from the touch, closing "their strange petals," and the prophet is a "woman on a nurse's arm" who screams "Hell, Devil, Hell" without stopping. Here, the "salmon-colored" walls are so bland, a visual echo of the "anemic blush" of houses in the suburbs beyond, that they cannot be told apart, spring cannot be distinguished from fall (autumn/spring he calls it) and the geese, startled by aimless passersby, fly up in a rush but don't know where to go—"To the north? To the south?" The destination doesn't matter as long as it is far from these endless walkways.

"The Swan" is Ekelöf's picture of the institutionalized terror of our regimented lives, the illness of bureaucratized souls, and the obscenity all real speech eventually turns to when lives are regulated. Created out of the sadness of Finnish heroics and the isolation of one in spiritual exile from his enemies and his people, it contains the ennui of botched encounters and missed connections. It is Ekelöf crossing the barren Lapland landscape by train, the sun forever low on the horizon. "Hell, Devil, Hell!" it shouts, the words a hollow echo, an empty lament—and yet. . . .

And yet, the poem ends this way:

> A freshness lives deep in me
> which no one can take from me
> not even myself.

"Midwinter spring is its own season," Eliot wrote. "En friskhet"—a freshness.

We know the fury—fury at nothing, fury at nothingness, fury that the world we look on today, its rocks and stones and trees, its wars and deaths and loves, is the same as yesterday. There is no story behind this anger, no conflict or plot worth mentioning, no reproach from Barbara, who was a bride twenty years ago and keeps the colors in my world even now, no hard words between us on this gray day, only the quotidian and its attendant ennui. The tilt of her head, endearing before, is only a tilt of her head this morning, and her words, always a surprise, surprise now in the same way.

Endless walks, walks circle, circle around, around bottomless, bottomless dams, dams endless. I pace the floor in front of the computer screen, my tread wearing familiar patterns in the carpet until I notice what I've often, uncomprehending, seen, my foot coming down on the silvered print it had left only moments before and—that's it!

I grab a scarf from the tottering coat rack, step into mud shoes, and head out, slamming the back door behind me, aware of Barbara in the picture window above, cradling her coffee cup in her hands as she does every morning in the manner I know as home and happiness but bear now as a mystifying burden, afraid to look back over my shoulder, stumbling as if drunk, though not drunk enough, down the path away from the maddening comforts of all that I love, past junk and mud and weeds and graves, a vaporous mumbled nonsense—"Hell! Devil! Hell!"—floating behind me in the cold like a scarf, and the dog trotting, oblivious, behind, damn tail wagging.

Then lake.
Then midday darkness.
Then, suddenly, snow.

What is the changed name of God in our time? Sometimes a walk around the lake in spring helps, the surface, locked in opaque glitter all winter, yielding at last to water, to the reflective, the passive, the powerful. "Oh I have walked around the lake," Logan writes,

> when I was not alone—
> sometimes with my wife have seen these swans
> dip down their necks
> graceful as a girl. . . .

The lake is St. Joseph's in South Bend where Logan taught, and it is visible over his shoulder in a photo taken in the early sixties, about the time that the poem was written. It is late fall or early spring in the picture, the trees bare, leaves scattered on the ground, and Logan, dressed for teaching in a tweed jacket, tie, dark slacks, and white socks, sits on a stump, his hands folded calmly—almost demurely—in his lap. He looks energetic and tense, more like the scientist he studied to be than the poet he was. Behind him the lake extends implacable and white—like the sky, like his forehead.

During one autumn walk around the lake, a student "found a perfect hickory shell" in the fall leaves and put its "white bread" into Logan's palm. Most of the time, though, Logan was the teacher that he could not help being. "I have much for which to thank John," wrote a student who was with him during these years. "He taught us self-amazement." Self-amazement was, unfortunately, the one lesson that Logan could not teach to himself. He drank too much, lost his family, and eventually lived alone on a houseboat. "With myself again," he writes, and adds parenthetically, "we hardly speak."

What is God's winter name? The lonely, exiled, war-weary Swedish poet, who had himself gone beyond cynicism, put a hickory shell in Logan's open hand in answer—the answer to all who find that the unclean spirit has returned to the well-swept house:

Ekelöf said there is a freshness
nothing can destroy in us
—not even we ourselves.
Perhaps, that
Freshness is the changed name of God.

Freshness. On the tape of Logan reading his poem aloud, the word sounds brisk and brittle—all short "e's" and sibilant "s's"—all *friskhet*, freshness.

"Hey look!" I shout, peeling off my coat in front of the picture window. I have just finished running up our road, eager to tell Barbara about the snow. "It's coming—whoa!—it's really coming down hard now!" I say, watching the snow dropping in fat wet flakes. I hear Barbara, off in another part of the house, singing. Suddenly the music stops, and I know she is watching too.

They are "bread," John Logan says, they are "manna," they are "bodies." Each flake, born of sky, grows by its clinging design until it is too sluggish to ride the winds and can do nothing but fall on carhood, fencerail, and bicycle seat and skid and dissipate in a rush or drift dreamily into grass and mulch and puddles and soak in with a sigh. Our window fills with them—a vision of verticals—oaks and pines and endless columns of white as all that rears skyward finds a way back to earth and is remade from the being of God into the image of God, the doily-hexagonal-star shape planted on a hickory stump like a generative kiss of death, a kiss that is first substance, then shape, and finally image on the way like us all to something new and something very, very old.

"Look," Barbara says kneeling beside me, gazing over the sofa back at a window of white. "They're big as two-by-fours!" I sink back on the pillows and, seeing her there, can't help smiling. I take in the nap of her sweater, the tilt of her head, and the way her fingers cradle the empty coffee cup—all the familiar stuff—but see them now as if for the first time. *Two-by-fours!* Where did she get that, I ask myself, in love all over again, the white wonder whirling about us?

Several days later, I take the call ("Better go by Dick's and get the chainsaw before you come home," Barbara says) and when I turn the corner of our road, saw and fuel container bouncing in the back floorboards of the Escort, I see what she meant: an enormous hickory trunk lies across the road, amid a wave of gray branches. I hack away at the small limbs first—they fall aside without resisting, my son working behind, gathering the debris and hauling it into the woods. Then, I turn the blade on the broad back of the trunk.

An odd detachment comes when I cut wood with a chainsaw, engulfed in the deafening whine, my arms numb and tingling from the shuddering machine, the world—all sound and touch gone—suddenly reduced to my field of vision. The blade floats before my goggles as it gnaws through tight-grained hickory, riding like a planchette along the groove it is making. I hang on, sweating through my jacket, alone in the saw's compass, the smell of burning hickory—a dry, pungent, winter musk—my only link to the world. In the midst of this raging serenity, Logan's poem comes to mind.

> And once on a morning walk
> a student who had just come back
> in fall found a perfect hickory shell
> among the bronze and red
> leaves and purple flowers of the time
> and put its white bread into my hand.

When the tree trunk falls free, rolling down the bank toward the creek, I cut off the motor, the silence of the woods crashing down around me, and set down the saw, my arms tingling and useless, rising weightless like wings.

When Odysseus washed up on the island of the Phaiakians and confronted the princess Nausicaä and her maidens, he was naked except for "a single branch of olive, whose leaves might shield him." His hair matted and skin mottled from days and nights asleep in the sand, he delivered his plea to the band of teenage girls, frightening the giddy maidens away. Only Nausicaä remained, and Odysseus had nothing to make her forget his naked body but his speech.

When Odysseus spoke, we are told, his words "poured forth like snowflakes."

Everywhere the small boats of the yard—acorn caps, flower pots, glider seats, and handlebars—carry cups of snow in their hollows. The bird feeder lifts its open face of white to the gray sky, the clothesline hauls snowy lumps across the garden, the stump wears its silly cap, and rhododendron along the bank stand stiffly in their ice epaulettes. The path down the slope to the creek digs a meandering curve of white through gray trunks, and the creek itself—stone-tossed, rock-churned, and foamy—rushes under icicles, like a thief getting away.

En friskhet.

"Statues only serve," one critic has written, "when their massive, self-contained materiality is denied." Only when the statue sheds its stone does it awaken. Midwinter spring is its own season. So John Logan—cold, drunk, and weary—takes his place then and forever in the arms of God among the barren statues of thieves, awaiting the gratuitous transformation of "the bronze Christ's brow and cheek." It is spring. It is winter. It is God's winter home where—now or never and always—snow blooms.

The Art of Translation

Writing essays is like realizing that you love your wife after all. We sing poems and dream fictions but speak in mere sentences. They are our friends, taken for granted, until one day a few singers and dreamers let go of all that is far away and, watching the face across the kitchen table, see for the first time in years a smile that was there all along, the smile of the girl they married, and learn in lowly prose how to want what they have.

Close your eyes and you can picture a poem as it takes its sinewy shape in the mind. It is seductive and memorable. The personal essay has a shape, too, and a certain loveliness about it, but walk away and try to picture it or describe it to a friend and you have little more than mousy-brown hair and cute freckles over the nose. Bookstores don't even know where to put collections of essays, lumping our shy girls in plain wrappers with how-to books and biographies that bear the slim, the rich, the wild, and the glamorous on their glossy covers.

In the ongoing battle to name the genre I prefer the venerable "personal essay" over other contenders, primarily because it lowers expectations. With "Creative Nonfiction" we are tempted to capitalize and court the grandiose. This is not just a fiction, the term announces. It's real! This is not just nonfiction. It's creative! You open a book of Creative Nonfiction ready for the best of all possible literary experiences—nothing ahead except disappointment. But with the lowly personal essay, the reader, expecting some dull tract, can be surprised.

The phrase "personal essay" is, I think, a pleasant mouthful. "Essay" is appropriately serious, coming from the Latin *exagium*, meaning to weigh, a reminder that essayists ponder and measure and take stock of the world by weighing their words carefully. It suggests thought, and without a modifier is, probably, a little too austere, conjuring up another word, "examination," with which it is too often linked, and bringing back memories of dreaded blue books, so the word "personal" is a happy addition. Putting the word "familiar" in front of "essay" is probably a little too cozy, giving a misleading suggestion of safety and shared assumptions, but adding the modifier "personal" says that, behind these words, is a human being—a unique recombination of dirt and water and sky.

What they are called matters less than what they do. "Good for what?"—that is my aesthetic. Poetry, of course, is good for nothing and proud of it, according to W. H. Auden. "Poetry makes nothing happen," he wrote, and whether he is right or wrong, we know what he means. The reaffirmation of mere beauty is enough and says something good about all who love poems. Personal essays, by contrast, are very busy, performing many jobs. They supply information, entertain, and provide flawless and therefore irksome models for millions of college students learning how to write decent prose, but their main business is the solitary soul in a changing world, a clear and valuable mission.

The personal essay is uniquely positioned for the task. Unlike the ceremonial and communal forms—poetry and drama—the essay came into its own recently, during the Renaissance, the era of great figures, and functioned as a vehicle for the voice of the individual, carrying on this hard work into our century, which still gives lip service to individualism but no longer believes that any one of us makes much of a difference. The novel, born at the same time, bears this burden as well, but does so by placing the hero among the contending voices of other characters in defining social situations. The personal essay, by contrast, is the lone voice.

The novel—with its party atmosphere—has always been the more popular form, leading envious essayists to ransack the house of fiction. Dialogue, scene, verbal high jinks, narratives, character development, juxtapositions, even fictions, are all in the essayist's repertoire of effects. Anything that is good in my essays is true, I like to tell people, and some of the best parts were invented.

And yet, an essay feels very different from the story. Fiction writers hunt for those details that seem striking and memorable and include these in stories and novels for effect. A novelist might describe a character who bolts machine parts and an electric fan to the hood of his car and drives through town. Such choices, whether they come from real life or not, seem made up precisely at the point that they achieve a memorable oddity. "I've got to put that in my next story!" we suspect the author has said, glad to come upon a detail that we cannot overlook. "Give your character a scar," I once heard Alice Walker tell a group of fiction writers, suggesting a way to make characters distinct. Essayists, drawn to the mundane rather than the sensational, tend to be suspicious of such scars.

A friend of mine who is an expert on the Romantic poets once told me that when Wordsworth and Coleridge used to walk through the Lake District of England together, they had radically different experiences. Coleridge did not see much around him. Instead, he allowed the landscape to stir his imagination and encourage invention, the walk giving him freedom to look within and examine interior states. Wordsworth, on the other hand, knew the names of wildflowers and trees and noted subtle changes in the landscape and season as he walked, looking outside himself for inspiration. The essayist is more like Wordsworth than like Coleridge, and the difference can be felt by reading "Tintern Abbey" and "The Rime of the Ancient Mariner" back-to-back.

It helps to have a dull life. Novelists, dreaming up other lives, can forget the mess they are making of their own as they create strange new worlds to fulfill the yearnings of this one. But personal essayists are never off duty, which makes even simple acts like showering, driving, or sex difficult if not dangerous. "Much is in little," Horace wrote, and essayists keep the job manageable by thinking for a long, long time about hardly anything at all, an uneventful life allowing the writer to care more about "what is" than "what happens." Desire is the subject of novels—not what I have, but what I want. Capable of glamour and often at odds with the world as God made it, the novel is the prince of prose and apt, at times, to do the devil's business. The essay is the lowly monk of literature, quietly going about God's work.

This reverence for the way things usually are marks the essay, though it is not a requirement of the form, and explains the elegiac nature of these works, which are recording a present that is continually slipping away, largely unnoticed. Perhaps that is why the form is congenial to the ends of civilizations—when an entire way of life is threatened—and offers a clue for why some of the earliest examples of the personal essay occurred in the Hellenistic period and later at the end of the Roman Empire.

"Getting it right" in fiction means something different than it does in an essay. Fiction tends to myth. Unwilling to claim a reality for its subject before the text, it becomes real only as it represents lives on the reader's side of the page. One way to get it right in fiction, then, is to make the tale convincing, a plausible sequence of surprises.

Essays, by contrast, begin with something that exists and has meaning before it reaches the page, assuming plausibility and establishing a different contract between the reader and the writer, a different set of literary obligations. Essays are not arranged by plot but by anxieties. They don't wonder "what next?" Instead, like a worried parent, they ask "*now* what?" with a groan. The anxieties are relieved not so much by the telling, like confessions, but by the arranging, the way some of us fix a problem at work by cleaning up the desk. "Getting it right" for an essayist means putting events and details into a revealing—a revelatory—relationship with each other. Strolling through the museum of love and change, the essayist rearranges for all to see the treasures we cannot keep.

These differences should not be pushed too hard. Essayists occasionally look up from the turtles and earthworms and moths of everyday life and bring the extraordinary into the lens of their prose, and essays do tell stories. "We tell stories in order to live," Joan Didion, an exact and exacting essayist, wrote, reminding us of the tenacity of the narrative impulse. But stories and essays are different in one crucial and revealing way, an essential difference inherent in the forms. The Pandora's box of fiction, unavailable to the personal essayist, is dramatic irony.

The novelist can create a character who speaks in the first person but does not share all—or any—of the author's views. The character becomes that infamous thing, an unreliable narrator, a literary tool that allows the author, as Joyce suggests about Flaubert, to be everywhere in a work and nowhere present at the same time. Novelists—masters of bad faith—often hide behind this device, usually making fun of the character who tells the tale for them, sometimes letting the readers in on the joke, sometimes not. This ironic edge is always in fact present in a first-person novel—we are, after all, the last to know the truth about ourselves. Flaubert even perfected a strategy of indirect address, an aping of a character's voice and attitude, which allows the author to create the same effect in third person prose. "Madame Bovary, c'est moi," he wrote. Don't believe it.

So, the governess telling the tale, in one famous example, may blame others for the demise of the children in her care, but we readers, upon whom nothing will be lost, catch the author's wink between the lines and suspect that the governess herself is, in fact, the guilty party. *Is* the author winking? On Monday, Wednesday, and Friday the governess is guilty as sin and duping us. On Tuesday and Thursday she seems more crazy than sinister and therefore guilty without knowing it. And on Saturday we bemoan our tendency to intellectualize every damn thing, pick up a hard ball and glove, and declare the poor woman innocent. Who knows? The screw turns and turns and turns, endlessly. It's a tricky and sophisticated game, the subject of great debate, and a mountain of literary criticism.

Irony of this kind obviously enriches a text, rendering the simplest tale suddenly subtle and ambiguous, and the writers of personal essays, by the nature of their task, cannot use the technique. Essayists lie and mislead and invent—who doesn't? In all ways except one they remain incorrigibly human and therefore thoroughly unreliable. But there is a lie that they cannot tell with a straight face: they cannot get any aesthetic distance on the narrator. If the essay is personal (and here I leave out some excellent essays by writers like Swift and Russell Baker, which are not personal in the way I mean), the distinction between author and narrator, by definition, collapses; they see the world eye-to-eye, so to speak. Who you read is what you get.

The personal essayist, by sacrificing the unreliable narrator, removes one tool for complexity from the literary arsenal but suffers no loss. Dramatic irony is the fictional tool that has turned literature in this century into a hall of mirrors. With the author everywhere absent—and God, as Joyce added, paring his fingernails—the reader is left alone in an era of great loneliness. Even when we read masters of these techniques—writers like Nabokov, for instance, in *Pale Fire*—we begin to suspect that literature in them is reduced to a game. It may be animated by a great heart, but we sense mainly an absence behind it all—the human being who is speaking the words so impeccably camouflaged that she or he might as well not be there at all.

In the personal essay, as Thoreau reminded us a century and a half ago in the opening page of *Walden*, we are stuck with the voice of the author, no intermediary. There are several ways for the writer to offer relief from the inevitable monotone. A mixed diction helps—Aristotle first taught us that, encouraging us to use the whole range of vocabulary that is available to the author's voice. The vulgar requires vulgarity, damn it, and the divine demands all the verbal splendor that the dictionary has to give. Many essayists use quotations as a way of clearing their throats before going on. First-person accounts in novels are often restricted to the speaking voices of the characters, but the first-person voice of the personal essayist can be, without strain, the speaking voice liberated by the reading mind.

A last resort—often required by the essayist whose voice is sounding shrill—is the joke. Out on the limb of a ridiculous proposition or situation, the essayist hands himself a saw. Self-deprecation is the essayist's most convincing tool—the equivalent in writing of comforting others by saying, "You think *that's* bad?" Such humor is not an evasion or a case of false humility, but a way of making readers feel less alone with their own foibles. And, of course, once we have laughed together, it is easier to talk.

Essayists have an arsenal of techniques like these for modulating without undermining the narrator's solo voice, ways of engaging in dialogue, which is the path, Socrates taught us, to wisdom, but that does not mean that the essayist can be, like the novelist, everywhere and nowhere at once in his work. "Here I am," the personal essayist says, like the Old Testament prophets when they were called, trembling, before God, and like the prophets the writer often feels like adding, "Oh Lord." Personal essayists may not have a thesis, a clearly thought-out position on the world's imponderables, but they are, at least, willing to stand, come what may, in the same verbal patch as the voice of the essay.

This limitation—the collapse of ironic distance—is chastening for any writer. "Say what you mean and mean what you say," my father used to caution in his firmly tautological way. "Discipline," according to Michel de Montaigne, the father of the personal essay, requires that "one is the same within, by his own volition, as he is outside for fear of the law and what people will say." It is true. In my own case, I have grown to distrust those who talk one way in public and another in private, their pieties in front of others followed by rib-poking obscenities over a beer in a backroom. I have grown to distrust myself when I act that way.

The joy in all this is that the reader of the essay is allowed to hear this voice play occasionally with an idea. Ideas haven't fared well in our century, and the prospect for the next century does not seem much better. Poets have, in essence, followed William Carlos Williams in abandoning them. "No ideas but in things," he wrote about poetry, contributing to the impoverishment of the form. Novelists put ideas on the lips of characters they don't trust and say to the reader, in essence, "you decide, I can't." That is why essayists turn the ideas over and over, considering possibilities, allowing for contradictions, aware that the blame will, eventually, fall their way. It is a relief, in fact a privilege, in our age of images and ideologies to follow these solitary minds, these questioning voices willing to offer tentative assertions that they hold as true — at times even self-evident — in context, a context that the essay, itself, generously supplies.

There is, out there in the world of readers, a longing for reality behind words. I see it manifested in the tendency of many to read fiction as biography, to study the author's picture on the covers of books for clues to the text, investing authors' works with their lives. The personal essay goes a long way toward meeting this longing not because it sticks to reality any more than the novel does — or the poem or the painting, for that matter. But the essayist *is* stuck with himself or herself, in sickness or health, for richer or poorer, till death — an indicator of the stakes. The essay may not be honest to God or the world, but it had better be honest to a voice.

Being at home in the world — that is the task. Essayists learn to live with what they have and who they are, poking fun at that yakking voice in the head, yes, but respecting it and attending to it as well. Something is always lost in translation, and it is easy to be ironic about what words can't catch. Learning to relax the irony requires an act of generosity, but we do it all the time. If we are generous and lucky when we hear an old tune, we can get past the sappy lyrics to a true emotion. Loving what we have, we find the girl in the wife, or, reversing the metaphor, see the fair-haired boy in the bald man snoring beside his glass of sherry in an easy chair across the room. Creating the possibility for such generosity on the part of readers is the unique work of the personal essay, the by-product of its art, and as it accomplishes this task, as it sets us up for loving all that we will lose, it helps us in the job of being human.

Blue Books

The melancholy name says it all. Blue books. Repositories of the memorized self, mementos of all that we have left undone and unlearned, soulless snapshots of the mind. In them we say what others have—more eloquently, more adequately—said, misreading the wisdom of the past to call it our own. Blue indeed. The shadow of our thought. The outline of our ignorance. Hours of reading, underlining, making lists, and formulating handy mnemonics brought to a crisis by twelve pages of white, lined paper wrapped in blue. "Composing at the point of utterance," I tell my students, quoting one of my teachers. "Bullshit," they say.

There is the question, passionless and loaded, customarily passed out with the sealed book or stacked in mimeo on the desk and taken nonchalantly by students whose pose of indifference is their last shred of dignity. "Consider," it insists, "indicate," or "compare," speaking of "causes" and "genres" and "sources" and bearing, like the stages of a fatal disease, grizzled names such as "midterm" and "final." Who knows which instruction is more chilling? Probably "analyze," with all its overtones of breakdown and mental illness. Nearly as treacherous, though, is "discuss"—directionless and apparently open-ended, like a swamp—its pits unknown.

> "Why do gods appear to Greeks in human form, usually as a friend? *Discuss*, using the appearance of Mentes to Telemachus in the *Odyssey* as a starting point. What relevance does this ancient attitude toward deity have for us today?"

Snapping the seals of their books, my students open to the first page, blink once or twice and stare blankly into their hands. *Discuss*—hmm. The affair begins, a one-night stand for some, a lovers' spat for a few, and a groveling and whoring for the rest.

This quarter I taught a class in the oldest building on campus—the room once belonged to the poet Byron Reece, a little-known but important writer from our area who attended the college and later taught here himself. All autumn I talked about Homer, Dante, and Shakespeare while the hand-shaped leaves of a maple outside my window glowed orange. Plots thickened, and leaves, blackening at the edges, curled into brittle fists snapping in the breeze. As literary heroes followed their blood to the ground, gusts cast up a whirl of color—"rust and flame" Reece called the sight—and all that fell came to rest in piles at the feet of desultory students kicking a path back to the dorms. Now, when I am passing out finals, the trees are bare, their brilliance gone.

Julia labors a full fifteen minutes or so over a test that will make up a third of her grade. Her jeans are tight, laced at the ankles. "I guess it takes you forever to get them off," I whisper as she hands in her test. "No," she says brightly—unflappable and without irony—"not at all," and waves goodbye, her perfect brown hair flipping at her shoulders as she dashes down the steps, an incongruous, paisley scarf about her neck blowing off her shoulders like a liquid breeze. A "liquefaction," the poet Robert Herrick called such pretty sights. What could a Julia know about gods and grief?

Several hours later the last Julia hands in her paper and dashes out the door, piling into a convertible filled with screaming classmates. Tires burn rubber as the car squeals once and races down the faculty drive, the roar of the motor reduced to a mere whispered hiss and eventually to nothing, the young leaving in their wake the fallen bodies of all our dead heroes.

The silence of winter break begins.

My favorite poem by Byron Reece has nothing to do with his usual topics: farming, mountains, and death. Called "In the Corridor," it is about exam day—"a day all dull and dun"—and describes students leaving after taking a final "on the eve of holiday." I like it, in part, because it takes place in this classroom, a room with two doors that face, as the poet writes, "on an open hall" so that "one may go by the way he came or not."

The teacher in the poem, obviously Reece, has had a student read a poem by Herrick aloud from a "ponderous book" and is still "caught in the spell" of the old poet's "youthful music" on a "youthful tongue." Dismissing the class, Reece follows "the laughing lot" into the hallway that offers several choices but, inevitably, points the students away from him. There is, the poem suggests, a gulf between the young who learn poems and those who have carried them for years in their hearts, and even the one student, shut out from his happy friends by a "grave, unsmiling face," cannot bridge the gap. The boy turns to see if Reece's "gaze sought his" and whether the teacher's mind was

> . . . still for the ageless music of Herrick, or
> For the aging day, or the book,
> Or for the face at the end of the corridor
> And its fleeting backward look.

His mind is, of course, on all these—the poem tells us so—but the words "fleeting" and "backward" are valedictory, the youth taking what he has learned into the corridors of the world, leaving the teacher behind with an ageless book and an aging day.

"Litera scripta manet," I like to tell my students, "the written word remains," and, reluctant to check out the script in their blue books, I wander through the empty rows of desks in the classroom reading the graffiti. Looking at these desktops, I see the written word also gives us away. "Joint Committee," one desk declares in bold print, a drawing of a cannabis plant beside it. "Go Nads Go," shouts another. "I love Tom," one student writes, "in Florida?" another asks, and "who cares?" adds a third. "Do you have any value of a human life," a philosopher, composing no doubt at the point of utterance, muses incoherently, and an illiterate preacher in the making admonishes us with "you reap what you sew."

Names. So many names. Kat, Jess, Taylor C, Phantom, Cread, Bonny, Booger, Baby Rich. Names familiar and names strange. One desk is signed, like the Declaration of Independence, by Licker, Pugsley, T.B., NOID, RAID, scammer, and Loggerhead. An anonymous "I" loves Mike and Michelle and Mindy and Miranda and Mark—just to list the "m's." There are the obscenities reminding the naive that wastes are still eliminated, fornication continues, and parentage at times is uncertain. Harvey sux, one desk shouts, going into some ugly details on the subject, and English sux, and so—dear God—does Emily Dickinson.

According to these desks, literature is not much on the students' minds—*they* are on their minds and in their dreams and at each other's throats, which is as things should be, but when I head back to my desk, the winter day all dull and dun about me, I feel hollowed out, emptied of them, and very separate from the living, haunted by the fleeting, backward look of names dug in wood. Reece called nostalgia the "sudden recognition of mortality," and looking at these desks—it's true—I wish I were dead. Where are Licker, Pugsley, T.B., and NOID? And why am I the punch line of their jokes? Come back Bonny and Booger and Baby Rich. We're at Loggerheads here, I'm going down, and no RAID, no scammer, can bring the Phantom back to life.

In 1938, when Reece was a student at the college, his teacher and mentor was W. L. Dance, or "Little Man," as the students liked to call him. Dance had heard of Reece before the young poet arrived. "A Reece boy who has already published poems in both *Harper's* and *Mercury* will be with us next year," he wrote to one of the members of the Quill, the literary club on campus. When Reece arrived, the Quill took him in.

Dance conducted the group informally, allowing students to sit in a circle and read poems aloud for comment. "The Little Man," one of the students later wrote, "would be as nice and helpful as he could." Dance was "the most wonderful and natural teacher I have ever known," one of the other professors on campus said, adding that it "was Mr. Dance who gave Byron the release he needed so that his infinite mind could range at will and pour itself out in song." The best kind of teacher, Dance pointed students to a world beyond himself. So, when Ralph McGill of the *Atlanta Constitution* visited the campus asking about Reece, it was Dance who walked the famous editor across the lawn to the shy boy's room and knocked on the door.

Twenty-seven years later an impoverished and tubercular Reece was teaching at the college himself and followed the Little Man one more time. After grading blue books and setting them in a neat stack in his desk, Reece put Mozart's Piano Sonata in D on the record player and shot himself in the left lung. No doubt his old teacher was on his mind, since he chose to commit suicide in the room where Dance—his mentor and his guide—had killed himself ten years before.

Litera scripta manet. Here's a sobering thought. Almost all that we have of Aristotle comes to us from student notes. The original dialogues have been lost, and the works that remain are course summaries edited by Aristotle and his followers, Aristotle's original words and the commentary of his students mixed in an impossible tangle. Critics in our century have spent a good deal of time anxiously sorting out who said what in these notes, but Aristotle, I suspect, would not have objected to the muddle.

Aristotle's teaching method, adapted from that of Socrates, was based on dialogue, which is in fact a kind of muddle. Classes at the Lyceum were conducted along a series of walkways, allowing the teacher to walk and talk while students trailed along behind. The peripatetic school, Aristotle called it, literally, the "walking around school." No one slept in those classes, the idea of "keeping up" taking on a definite meaning. With students literally following in their footsteps, the teachers at the Lyceum had a clear sense of a continuum, a visual image of lives in the service of ideas that are passed on and transposed, the individual self, the leader for now, eventually abandoned along the way.

What after all is dialogue but a letting go of self, our ideas altered, misconstrued, and becoming themselves at the point of someone else's utterance? What is an honest question except a relinquishment of control, the subjection of a cherished belief to the scrutiny of others? *Discuss,* we write and watch our ideas go to gabble in the hopes that one day they may, by the alchemy of discourse, turn to gold. In the *Meno,* Socrates teaches a boy geometry by resisting the urge to explain. Eventually he taught his disciples—and the world—by letting go of his life, and taking his place in the pantheon of pure forms.

In Dante's *Inferno,* the only truly loving portrait of a sinner is Dante's description of a teacher, Brunetto Latino, the author of the *Tresor,* a book that Dante drew upon to write his works. In the passage, the teacher asks that his sinful life be forgotten and that he be remembered instead for his work, and Dante lets him have his say, crowning him with laurels for that matter, but, it must be remembered, he does put the old teacher in hell, making him run over a scalding desert with other sinners, and—the more telling rejection—he surpasses the teacher's encyclopedia by refashioning his fussy compendium into a masterpiece.

Teaching is the knife. With it we cut the future free and slide to our doom, taking little more than a fleeting backward glance for our reward. What is our legacy? Names scratched onto desks? Words marked and graded and stacked in a drawer? Or something worse—much worse. What do our blue books hide? Oh yes, blue books, I think with a shrug, reminded that the afternoon is late, and I haven't graded a single exam yet. Once again I start back to the stack of tests waiting to be marked, running a hand over scarred desktops, when one name in wood catches my eye: Audrey Terry.

Polite, brunette, and angelic, Audrey was an English peer tutor at the school in the 1970s. One of the prettiest students ever to attend the college, she probably did more for male literacy on campus than the entire English faculty. Boys flocked to her tutorials. Looking at the name, I see her plainly, the puzzled expression of faint surprise on her face when three boys gathered around her on the way to the dining hall, one boy walking in front trying to get her attention, and she, never coy, but shy, demurring.

I remember, too, a time that she was late for an eight o'clock class with a teacher who was notorious for locking the door at the second bell. Racing across campus, books hugged up to her front, she cut across the lawn, leaping an ankle high chain, but—grace undone — caught her toe and sprawled, unceremoniously, into the grass, books, papers, and beautiful girl brought down hard. Frowning at the windblown pages, she got up on her knees — no sense hurrying now, the late bell ringing — and looked sheepishly my way across a decade and a half.

"God does not exist — she happens," I wrote recently to a student who had been struggling with theological questions. My answer took me back to my own student days when, troubled by the question of God's existence, I talked to my Old Testament professor, Phyllis Trible. Only a little older than we were, Dr. Trible was without a doubt the most intense scholar at the college, speaking with an authority that left us trembling. If anyone had the answers, it was this woman, who on most days wore an oxford blouse, dark blue skirt, and penny loafers — and spoke with the spirit of God.

We met in the snack bar, a small, glass table between us, and her eyes, which in class went from student to student with easy and vague recognition, suddenly gazed at me alone, a dark steady beam.

"I don't believe God exists," I stammered.

"Oh," she said, registering no surprise. She had been through this before. "Which God?"

"Their God. Your God, I guess."

I had taken a philosophy course on the existence of God and knew all the gloomy answers. So, I rambled on for half an hour or so about man creating God and other blasphemies. I had wanted her to fight me and had hoped to God that she would win. Wisely, she refused, listening but not arguing. Eventually, I said all I knew on the subject and sat before her, silent at last, looking into my folded hands.

Always the teacher, she suggested a list of readings: Blake, Rilke, Langden Gilkey, Kierkegaard, and Martin Buber. She was teaching a course in cosmology the next semester — a seminar for seniors and I was a sophomore—but she would try to get me in. Soon—too soon—it was time to go, but seeing I was still upset, she spoke softly to me. "You've got all the answers," she said, leaning forward, the scholarly robes dropping away from her voice. "Maybe—just maybe—you're asking the wrong questions."

In the *Odyssey*, Athena appears to Odysseus' son, Telemachus, in the disguise of Mentes, a sea captain and family friend from a neighboring town. The disguise is not just to fool the lustful suitors who eat and drink greedily from the family provisions and lust after Penelope. It is for Telemachus, too—Athena's attempt to encourage boldness without frightening the boy. For his part, Telemachus is prepared, ready to leave his childhood behind and meet the best of himself in the form of a goddess who will send him on his own odyssey. While retainers wipe down tables and butcher whole carcasses for roasting, Telemachus, "who dreamed in the crowd," caught the eye of the goddess.

"God does not exist—she happens." It is, I see now, the answer to my essay question.

Eventually I do walk back to my desk and, as the window darkens beside me, work my way through the stack of blue books. The last shall be first, I think, getting to Julia's exam at the bottom of the stack. But what about the first?

> Sometimes my life is such a mess that I just fall down and cry. I'm like Penelope with all those suitors and their dirty jokes. Then a friend says something nice and gives me a hug, and the bad stuff just goes away, like that, and as long as the hug lasts I think my friend is Jesus. Sorry that's all I know. I hope it's what you want?

At the bottom of the page she added a postscript: "Merry Christmas."

I thought of the God who was a rabbi and walked among people teaching in parables intended to confuse the mighty and the wise. I thought of Julia, unlacing the legs of her jeans. I thought of a boy set apart from his friends by a sad face and another boy leaving his old answers behind, the voice of a goddess still ringing in his ear. Well, I wondered, reading the blue book again. What *do* I want? Then I remembered the mischievous glint in my teacher's eye when she said, "maybe — just maybe."

"Damn," I thought, flipping through the empty pages of Julia's blue book, "she got it right," and I gave the answer an "A."

"Love the questions," I like to tell my students, quoting Rilke, "because," I add, "you may not be able to live with the answers." So I drop the stack of blue books in a box and decide on a winter walk to the gazebo just beyond the maple tree, gladly leaving the answers behind. Unlike all the other buildings on campus that are named for wealthy benefactors, this airy spot is dedicated by members of the class of 1930 in "loving memory of their teachers." Set among dogwoods and several enormous oaks, it is shady during spring and summer and fills each autumn with leaves of flame and rust.

If you walk into it, you see in the beams overhead the names of former teachers, some of them still legendary on campus: Dr. J. A. Sharp, Deah Miller, E. L. Adams, Mary Cantrell, Wilma Coleman, S. B. Tolar, and others. Reece is not here, but Dance is, W. L. Dance, the "Little Man." Often I come here, at lunch or in the afternoons and, as students pass by on their way to classes, take comfort in the names carved in wood, harboring a secret hope that some day my name will be there too. Long after the desks are cleaned of graffiti — new blank slates for new students — the gazebo will remain. It is fitting. Students come and go, armed with our inadequate answers, while we stay behind with a stack of blue books and questions that will not go away.

The Gazebo

Like a motionless cat I hide in the center of things. Students, intent on where the sidewalk takes them, stroll by chattering, without noticing me. Talk of their joys and woes precedes them as they approach and floats like a banner behind when they pass—no whispering, no attempt to conceal the latest about parties and new loves and fresh failures. In the gazebo I am part of the scenery and easily overlooked in the way that mountains and sky become familiar and disappear.

The names of former teachers, carved in wooden beams, circle overhead, but anyone else who comes here is instantly rendered anonymous, and that's as it should be. The gazebo is about beyond. A humble house of open windows, it asks us to do the essential work of life — to look within by looking away.

There is much to see. Walkways that begin here crisscross a field dotted with dandelions and meander under fluted crowns of dogwood and oak. On the lawn, shirtless young men throw frisbees and women sunbathe, tipping their dark glasses occasionally, while at the edge of the playing field dormitories cast shadows over the glowing scene, gloomy, foreboding oblongs. I look past all of this — people, landscape, and shadows — my gaze settling at last on the shaggy side of a mountain dotted here and there with crags and bald patches, the end of my world. The gazebo calls us to gaze at the horizon.

In time, the horizon answers. Titmice and chickadees come unbidden, and shouts cast blithely on the dusky sky echo off of hills and return humbled by distance, the voices beyond me leaving plenty of room for the voice inside. The gazebo is a circle that shapes the universe into a halo, the heavens becoming geocentric again as I stare off in all directions. No matter how I have felt about the day, I am happy here. This is where I belong, I think, watching as the frisbee is tucked in with the books and the day folds up its quilt and slips on a dark sweater.

I come here for the same reason that I fish. An angler looks hard into the lake, intent on the day's catch gliding beneath the surface, only to find the sun and moon reflected there, instead, and his own hat lit by a nimbus. In fact, fishy metaphors often come to me in the gazebo, but along these lines I have some good news. The obligatory fishing essay, the one that got away from my first book, has slipped off the hook again in my new one — which is a surprise. Every personal essayist has to write an essay about fishing sometime, right?

Last summer I inherited Dad's tackle, a box of plugs and spoons and spinners with names like Bayou Boogie, River Runt, Mud Bug, Dardevle, Leadbelly, Salty Dog, Reflex Ripple, Rooster, and Beer Can. I usually opt for the venerable plastic worm with a hook in it, the fliptail or tube. Someday I hope to try them all, though there is a grizzly looking spiked and nameless thing at the bottom of the box — my little kraken — that I haven't touched yet. Lures. In this book about imitations, how could I resist the seductions of an essay on bait, I wonder? But I did.

Sitting in the gazebo is like taking a spot on a dock, casting the unbaited line of sight deep and waiting forever on the bobber of the spirit. It is the perfect place to compose the obligatory fishing essay, and sinking the hook just beyond the horizon I feel the tug in my own gut, but inevitably before the day is out I undo the mind's catch and let it go with a shrug and a sigh, bringing home little more than myself and an empty stringer.

I come to the gazebo often and at odd times. At night, the prospect is dotted with lights, like a decorated tree, the concrete floor crisscrossed with skeletal shadows. Squirrels clatter on the roof overhead and bats or swifts — I can't tell which — flit nearby, never really visible but registering on the retina as an afterimage, like traces of some unnameable guilt. One night years ago, when we lived just over the hill, and I couldn't sleep, I came to this spot in my robe, sat on the bank — there was no gazebo then — and stayed for hours, as the venom of insomnia worked its way through my system. At dawn I slipped back to the house unseen, in time to greet everyone at breakfast with a smile.

But the gazebo, as the name suggests, is built for the eye and comes into its full glory by day. The word began as a joke, formed in the eighteenth century by adding the Latin suffix "ebo," meaning "I shall," to the English word "gaze." Gazebo: I shall gaze. Some argue that the word is Oriental, and though there is no evidence for that, the notion is attractive because the act of sitting still and looking far off at nothing seems alien to the frenzy of our days — and something we need. In the gazebo, I set aside problems and take up imponderables. Shedding today in favor of forever, I trade all that comes to hand for vast distances, stepping out of time altogether and locating myself firmly in everywhere. When I die I hope my children will cast my ashes over this railing that has fitted me so well for worlds other than my own.

A house away from home, the gazebo is both clearing and bower, the wide sky just out of reach — an invitation to become the best in ourselves. At Thanksgiving this year, I noticed beside one of the posts a dime, put there for all to see. Throughout Christmas break the dime stayed in place, and once, after a dusting of snow, I brushed it clear. All winter quarter it remained, though I imagine those who spotted the coin could not resist picking it up and turning it over, marvelling at the universe's capacity for simple generosity, before setting it back on the railing. Today, in the midst of spring I checked, and it was gone, having lasted five months at the hands of us all.

Perhaps no one saw the dime, and that is why it stayed in place so long, the lovers in the gazebo drawn to flesh, not glitter, the rest of us looking beyond the railing for our rewards — "Ebo gaze." Those who did catch the glint of silver may have realized, perhaps — in this place of realization — that leaving it behind is more important than anything it could buy. What good is a dime in a gazebo except as a gift, an unspoken lesson to the next lucky soul who doesn't need it.

A gazebo is a glimpse of where we all are headed — our last challenge. "It's *not* a playhouse," my daughter, Alice, told me firmly one lazy spring afternoon when I tried to get her to entertain herself there. She should know. Recently, the college put on a production of *Three Little Pigs*, and when it was over my friend Dale Cochran, the artist who designed the set, gave Alice the pick of the pig houses. Having seen the show — and taken its lesson to heart — Alice chose well, and a few days later Dale and I delivered to my living room a twelve-foot replica of a brick house made of plywood. The playhouse was too tall, so we cut it in half, using the bottom as a side wall with a door, and arranged the house in the corner of our basement where Alice disappears for hours on end chattering merrily to herself, secure against parents and her brother, not to mention wolves.

A house within a home, a playhouse is where life's chores become fun. Alice lines things up in there but does so selectively, making a neat row of dishes while she sits on a mangle of stuffed animals, or lying down in a mangle of dishes to get her dolls in a row. Replicas allow Alice to step back from the everyday, though they contain in their physical reality enough of the stubbornness of things to keep her tied, by a tether of toys, to life. Her crossed eyes within inches of her doll's tiny accessories, she hoards her treasure of miniature shoes and souls, inviting into her life as many households as she can imagine—as long as they fit into the only home she has.

The gazebo meets a different set of longings. Unlike the playhouse, it does not point us toward the everyday. Rather, it looks away. If the playhouse is a cozy enclosure of painted walls, the gazebo is all windows, constructed out of emptiness and built for goodbye. A perch on the universe, it is a place to go when we put away childish things.

Of course, the gazebo itself is not necessary. We can walk into any clearing or lose ourselves in the woods, slowly turning about under a canopy of trees, taking in what is simply there. A lake is nice, the bobber playing hide and seek before our eyes in the glimmer of rippling water while our spirits, shy and unacknowledged, follow the rod skyward. All we need is a spot alone in the mere world. Even a cigar on the porch will do.

Mereness, of course, is problematic. Nothing merely is. There is a framing here that we cannot avoid, since the eye, like the hand, shapes all in its gaze, leaving prints everywhere. But if frames are unavoidable, then this house that is all frame, and little but a frame, will have to do. I do not shed myself here in the presence of oak and towhee or become "one with nature" in any sense of the phrase I can understand. Alone here but never lonely I feel simply human, which is as simple as I get and simple enough.

Being simply human is, in fact, hard these days—and getting harder, in part because the way humans know the world is changing radically. According to one expert, "A" will fall to "B"—a lower grade in my book—as atoms give way to computerized bits of information and the world is brought to us online and onscreen. In the electronic shopping mall that our world is becoming, simple reality will inevitably give way to its virtual stepcousin, the television a mere harbinger of a more insubstantial world—a phantom future—where all hungers are sated, but bodies and souls never fed. By the glow of a neon horizon, tooth and claw will be filed down to bytes according to the *lex digitalionis* of our faux new world. Even here, beside a gazebo on the campus of one of America's smallest colleges in the midst of southern Appalachia, workers wearing yellow hard hats are digging trenches and laying fiber optics cable, linking us, as our college president likes to say, to the world and beyond.

I consider myself lucky to live in a time when our imitations—our translations of life—are still, by and large, crudely atomic: wood and paint and breath and print on the page, all that crumbles and rots. We don't cheat death so easily, the weightiness of mere matter reminds us. The opportunity to be alive in the real world before we die is the only revenge. So, after all the cable has been laid and buried and reality comes to us through the mind before it reaches our fingertips, I hope that a few sanctuaries slip through the digits, an outdoors *off*line somewhere: a grove, a clearing, and an obligatory pond where a true line can be cast on thin air. Failing that, a gazebo would be nice, a hiding place at the center of wherever it sits, with a dime that nobody needs on the railing.